43-96   BK Bud   Sep-96

Praise for
Out Front Leadership

"In a field overpopulated with long, theoretical tomes, *Out Front Leadership* stands out as a valuable contribution from an author with real-life, take-charge credentials."

> EDMUND FALTERMAYER
> BOARD OF EDITORS
> *FORTUNE MAGAZINE*

"A must for any corporate decision maker. Combining the theoretical and practical, it is direct and to the point. It provides a clear understanding of what leadership is, as well as how to develop leadership in yourself and those around you."

> G. WALTER CHRISTOPHERSON JD, CPA
> LINSCOMB & WILLIAMS

"A practical presentation of the key components for developing and delivering strong leadership. Its positive, straightforward approach makes sense for both the public and private sectors."

> ANN W. RICHARDS
> GOVERNOR OF TEXAS

Praise for
Out Front Leadership

"Makes the messages about life and work we would like to pass on to the next generation understandable without sugar-coating. I'm sending copies to my children and plan to read it again myself each year."

JOHN P. (JACK) KELLY
PRESIDENT
GOODWILL GAMES, INC.

"As an executive search consultant, this book is enormously helpful in quantifying what has been 'gut feel' assessments. It succinctly tackles the definition and 'how-to' of the most important characteristic required by movers of American society and corporations—leadership!"

JAMES D. MEAD
PRESIDENT
JAMES MEAD & COMPANY

"Excellent for personal self study and a seminar workbook. The author's strong background lends credibility to the contents."

PETE M. HANNA
CHAIRMAN/CEO
HANNA STEEL CORPORATION

OUT FRONT LEADERSHIP

Cover Photograph: Dougal Haston out front,
leading an expedition to the summit of Mount Everest
(from *Himalayan Climber,* by Doug Scott),
photo by Doug Scott.

OUT FRONT
LEADERSHIP

Discovering, Developing, & Delivering Your Potential

JOE REYNOLDS

Mott & Carlisle

A BARD PRODUCTIONS BOOK

OUT FRONT LEADERSHIP
Discovering, Developing, and Delivering Your Potential
Copyright © 1994 Joe Reynolds

    Mott & Carlisle
    5275 McCormick Mountain Drive
    Austin, Texas 78734
    512-266-2112
    FAX 512-266-2749

ISBN 0-9636391-0-2

The author may be contacted through:
    Leadership Dynamics, Inc.
    4314 Cypresswood Drive
    Spring, Texas 77388
    713-353-3155

A BARD PRODUCTIONS BOOK
AUSTIN, TEXAS

    Editing: Jeff Morris
    Proofreading: Doris Dickey
    Text Design and Jacket Design: Archetype, Inc.
    Composition/Production: Archetype, Inc.
    Index: Linda Webster

Contents

PART ONE

Discovering Your Leadership:
The Critical Questions

PART TWO

Developing Your Leadership:
The Seven Characteristics of a Positive Leader

PART THREE

Delivering Your Leadership: Action for Contribution

Dedication

To my wife, Dyanne.

To Pierre Greeff, M.D.,
and the staff of the Stehlin Cancer Foundation
for their noble and unrelinquishing battle
on her behalf.

Acknowledgements

Out Front Leadership is the culmination of years of learning, experience, and the contributions of all those mentioned in the book and many who are not.

Special thanks to the people who helped turn my manuscript into the book you have in your hands. My secretary, Rebecca Williams, worked with me through several generations. The professional team at Bard Productions provided superior service all along the way. Jeff Morris through his insightful editing made it a better book. Archetype brought it to life with jacket and text design.

About the Author

Joe Reynolds has learned and experienced leadership from the ground up — by following, leading, and studying it since he was a Boy Scout. He has been a ditch digger, a "grunt" — and sergeant of grunts — in the Marine Corps, a construction supervisor, and a sales manager with the Procter and Gamble Company for 30 years. He has a bachelor's degree in industrial management from Samford University.

Reynolds is the founder of Leadership Dynamics, Inc., providing speeches and seminars on leadership for clients nationwide. He and his wife Dyanne have two grown children and live near Houston.

PART ONE

DISCOVERING YOUR LEADERSHIP

The Critical Questions

Who is crazy? Am I crazy because I see the world as it can be?
Or is the world crazy because it sees itself as it is?
—MIGUEL DE CERVANTES, DON QUIXOTE

These are exciting times to be alive! Our era is one of unending and rewarding change—transition encompassing, yet surpassing, the ages of agriculture, industry, and space. Ours is the era of the power of choice—the power to be the predominant creative force in our own lives. It is a time for people who are "can do-ers," "why not-ers," and "what if-ers"—people who will lead the "no can-ers," "not now-ers," and "yes but-ers" from self-imposed mediocrity toward opportunity and significance. It is a time for leaders to lead!

The young rebel against leadership; the old reflect on it; and everyone questions it. Part I of *Out Front Leadership* addresses the most common and critical questions about leadership.

Considering Leadership:
Can Sparrows Be Leaders?

There is very little difference in people, but that little difference makes a big difference. The little difference is attitude, the big difference is whether it is positive or negative. —W. CLEMENT STONE

Sparrows, the most common and ordinary of all birds, have a human counterpart: Harry Truman. Truman did not graduate from college, failed in his venture as owner of a clothing store, and was an unheralded, political machine–supported compromise as vice president of the United States. His recognized achievements were few until he became president in 1945 upon the death of Franklin Roosevelt. Yet, during his seven years as president, he soared like an eagle to become recognized as a decisive leader in national and international affairs.

Margaret Mead was a sparrow! James Michener referred to Mead as "sawed off, dumpy, red-faced, scraggly-haired, antagonistic, and remarkable." She called herself a "sacred whore," not because of sexual proclivity, but because she combined anthropology and psychology: she linked cultures and people. Margaret Mead and Harry Truman were two common sparrows who became uncommon leaders by influencing others through their positive self-image and action.

Self-image and leadership development begin in early childhood. Because it is easier and because they lack experience, children usually base their image of themselves on their socioeconomic status, physical abilities, and attractiveness—how they think others see them. Some people fail to grow beyond this immature self-image. They do not understand that the character of the whole is greater than the sum of its parts. Like each of us, Truman and Mead were not perfect in every way, but the sum of their character made them leaders.

My wife and I wrote the following fable to help others understand and develop their leadership abilities.

FOLLOW THE LEADER

Nine knighted birds meet with King Eagle at the Council of Flat Rock to discuss the future.

EAGLE: Welcome, my friends and fellow birds from near and far. I have called this meeting to tell you that I am no longer able to be your leader. My wings are old and grey, and they will no longer carry me to the great heights of freedom I so enjoy. My eyes now have the power to see only the largest of prey, while my talons have the strength to catch only the slowest and weakest. I still have much to offer to you and your young, through teaching and coaching; but no longer will my body fly through mighty storms when you need a leader the most.

All of you are different in your own way, for the Great Spirit made no two of us exactly alike. Each of you brings unusual talents and strengths to our team, but today we must select the one of you who, by example, shows the highest of standards.

CROW: Old Eagle, how can it be anyone but me? I stand out in a crowd; and when I light upon a tree, the others make room for me.

OWL: Yes, you stand out, Crow, but it is because you are a bully, and your cackling is gossip which only hurts others. You are lazy, for you really don't care; you live not by challenges, but by foolish dares. Instead, the leader should be me! The world calls me wise, for among all of you I am the most aware. Look how my head turns in all directions so there is nothing I don't see.

SPARROW (*thinking*): I am the most common of birds, and no one has ever told me that I am unique, or that I have any talent. I have always been jealous of Crow because he is not shy, and he is very smart—for he can count all the way to four. And Owl does see a lot, and he supposedly knows everything; but seldom does he share his ideas or feelings. I don't know what to think.

HAWK: I must be the leader! Eagle and I are of the same family; I should inherit the job! We are mighty hunters, and courage is our strength. There has never been a leader who was not as brave as we.

SPARROW (*thinking*): Miss Hawk is certainly brave, but doesn't she see that courage is shown in more ways than being a mighty hunter? I eat only seeds and worms, but yesterday I pecked the head of that sneaky fox who was trying to catch my little sister.

REDHEADED WOODPECKER: Miss Hawk, I agree that to be brave is needed, but what good is courage without a commitment to something other than your growing stomach? I, the Woodpecker, have promised to get rid of the killer bugs within our beautiful trees. Yes, I eat the bugs for food, but my promise is to save our trees. How can we have a leader who doesn't keep promises?

OWL: You silly redhead! Your brain is scrambled like eggs from your foolish pecking on trees. You don't kill enough bugs to save any of the trees.

SPARROW (*thinking*): Gosh, at least Red is committed to a goal that is important to something greater than himself. Besides, a lot of little ripples in the water can make big waves. What would happen if more of us had a goal like Red? Also, I am beginning to worry about Owl, for he is looking at the bad points in others before he looks for the good.

SWAN: Come on, look at the one who stands out the most — look at me! I am the queen of honesty and purity. Without honesty, there is no trust, and without trust, where are we? I trust even the spirit of rain, and enjoy her showers upon my pretty feathers. The rest of you just complain as you get wet before you hide in your nests. You hide from each other and you hide from yourselves—you hide from truth.

DOVE: My, my, Lady Swan, you sure do brag. I certainly agree on honesty being needed, but you show more love for yourself than for others. Our world will not have peace unless we care for and share with one another. When I was a baby dove, my parents taught me a major rule for leadership: "Do unto others, and yourself, as you would have others do unto you." You need to show more love and understanding, Lady Swan.

SPARROW (*thinking*): Both Swan and Dove show very good leadership qualities, Swan with her honesty, and Dove with his loving and caring. But just last week, I scolded my children when they stole worms from a playmate. I forgave them, and told them to share their food with him. Yet I never before thought of myself as being honest or caring.

HUMMINGBIRD: None of you has a body as small and frail as mine, yet look at all that I can do with it. I have grown my wings to go so fast and strong that I can fly in any direction, or even in just one place. Of all of us, I am the most confident in myself because I have overcome greater problems. We all know that our leader must be confident like me.

MOCKINGBIRD: Goodness, you are confident, Hummingbird! But surely you see that there are others with leadership skills that you don't have. I am by far the best talker. I can copy the speech of many birds, and I can also talk with dogs and frogs. To be a leader of freedom and peace for all, you must be able to talk with those much different from you.

SPARROW (*thinking*): Confidence and the ability to speak one's ideas are needed for leadership, and I have both. I am small, only five inches high, and I left my parents' nest when I was but two weeks old. The school of life has made me strong, and my mistakes have made me even stronger. I am happy, and I

19

share my joyful thoughts with sweet sounds of song as the sun sets. Other creatures listen to me.

EAGLE: Sparrow! Sparrow! Are you asleep? We did not invite you just to sit there! You come from the largest of all bird families, and surely you see that even sparrows are not all alike in every way. You have much in common with these other knighted birds, yet you have something different and valuable to offer them. Why are you so shy and quiet with these bragging birds?

SPARROW: Old Eagle, today, for the very first time, I realize that I am much like yet somewhat different from the rest. Yesterday, I thought a few were born to be leaders while the rest of us were not. I thought all leaders had to be brilliant and the best at everything. Today, I see that leaders are self-made through adversity—learning, winning, losing and winning again—all with the help of hero and heroine teachers.

Each of you claims to be the best in only one of the strengths required for leadership, but none of you claims to be even good in the rest. Think of what you have said:
- Crow is the smartest.
- Owl is the most aware.
- Hawk is the most brave.
- Woodpecker is the most committed.
- Swan is the most honest.
- Dove is the most caring.
- Hummingbird is the most confident.
- Mockingbird is the best talker.

I may not be stronger than you in any of your respective strengths, but I am stronger than any one of you in all of the strengths. My feathered friends, you may not choose me to be your new king and leader; but today, I choose to become the leader I believe I can be, and I offer myself to be *your* leader.

OWL: Old Eagle, can we recess before we vote? Sparrow has taught us several lessons today:

1. Leaders are made, not born. It is the pupils, who are learning, who will bring freedom and peace. The ones who know it all still live in yesterday.
2. Leaders search for the good, not the bad.
3. Leaders choose to believe that "the me I see is the me I can be."

Sparrow has given us much to think about.

As with the sparrow in this fable, attitudes are demonstrated by action; and action begins with each of us, each new day.

What is tomorrow without today?

Tomorrow is always tomorrow.

If we cannot live in the present, how can we live anywhere?

To live today is to discover and to act.

Whether to correct or to construct, today we must act to disrupt the status quo.

Risking together—

On the crest, and in the quest, of tomorrow.

Leadership:
Definitions and Dynamics

The challenging need of America is leadership—
people who have ability and reliability enough to carry
responsibility in business, in government, in church,
everywhere. Leadership can only be learned by leading.
—BOY SCOUT HANDBOOK

Attitude and action are two of the most evident separators between the common many and the uncommon few; but what is this thing, this term that identifies the uncommon few—leadership?

LEADERSHIP DESCRIBED

Leadership is tangible, yet intangible. You can see it, feel it, and market it for profit; and its gain comes not without pain. It is difficult to define, and to my knowledge, there are few words for it in non-English-speaking cultures (85% of the world's population). As with truth, where black and white are often muted into grey, it is an amalgam of extremes and ambiguities. Leadership surpasses doing what is right personally; it encompasses getting others to willingly do what is right. Having read this, do you have a definition for leadership?

During my years of studying and teaching the subject, I have read and heard many leadership descriptions, among them:

- A responsibility, rather than a privileged rank.
- The impact of me upon we.
- Responsibility *for* yourself
  and *to* others.
- The judgement to do what is right, the desire
  to transform, and the ability to educate.
- Getting extraordinary results through
  ordinary people.
- The force that makes you follow a person
  to a place you would not go by yourself.
- ". . . making real your full potential and
  helping others to do the same." (ABRAHAM MASLOW)
- "The bonding that holds together the few
  who plan and the many who implement." (LEO TOLSTOY)
- "The merchant of hope." (NAPOLEON BONAPARTE)

All of these are good descriptors, but separately they leave me wanting more insight. I struggled many years to develop a personal definition of leadership; in so doing, I was required first to discover the supreme vision of positive leadership. My conclusion was, and is, that the purpose of leadership is to bring about responsible and productive freedom for the betterment of humankind—a vision of unlimited potential and demanding challenge!

LEADERSHIP DEFINED

Positive leadership is striving toward a personal vision of excellence by working cooperatively through others. Positive leadership includes—

- responsible and productive individual action by the leader and followers.
- contribution to one's self, community, organization, country, and all humankind.
- leader and followers doing what they want to do while becoming who they want to be.
- risk and sacrifice.

There is no real gain without pain, no real getting without giving, no real success without setbacks, no real reward without contribution.

Abraham Lincoln personified this definition, as did the less-known Sioux Indian Chief Sitting Bull. Sitting Bull did much more than defeat General Custer.

> *Through his courageous focus on commitment, trust, and teamwork, he rallied the many proud and independent Sioux tribes around a single banner—rekindling the greatness of his people.*
>
> —EMMET C. MURPHY

Drayton McLane, Jr., is a less familiar contemporary example of my definition of leadership. McLane's early-on vision was to become the foremost supplier of goods to convenience stores in the U.S. and, concurrently, to contribute to the nation, and to society at large, his leadership principles and innovations in his industry. He expanded his father's wholesale grocery business from a small warehouse in Cameron, Texas, into an international business with 18 distribution centers and a 1991 annual sales volume of $3.7 billion. His employees regularly work ten-hour days, yet the employee avoidable-turnover rate is among the lowest in the industry.

His associates and competitors have acknowledged his leadership by electing him to lead various industry boards of directors as well as the Baylor University Board of Regents, and by making him national chairman of the Children's Miracle Network. Currently he is a vice chairman of Wal-Mart and the owner of the Houston Astros baseball team.

LEADERSHIP IN TRANSITION

The dominant principle of organization has shifted, from management in order to control an enterprise to leadership in order to bring out the best in people and respond quickly to change.
—JOHN NAISBITT AND PATRICIA ABURDENE

The concept of leadership is undergoing a major transition. The predominant thrust of leadership through the 1950s was autocratic, often militaristic, establishing an environment of compliance, exactness, and conformity. It was an era of command leadership by a few, with emphasis on results today and little regard for tomorrow. General educational levels were low. Jobs were mostly in agriculture and industry.

Today's leaders are faced with new generations of followers who have grown up differently from their predecessors. They are better educated, better informed, and more independent in thought and attitude. They manipulate information and provide services in more democratic, less hierarchical organizations. Raised in an era of growing awareness of human, civil and economic rights, they have higher expectations for the quality of their life. Although sometimes more difficult to motivate and lead, many have high potential for becoming effective leaders.

> *I suppose leadership at one time meant muscles;*
> *but today it means getting along with people.*
> —INDIRA GANDHI

Leadership is the choice of becoming over being, contributing over receiving, positive change over status quo. Leadership opportunities thrive in all roles at all levels within our society, and none is more important than that of becoming a responsible parent. Adults, as well as children, apply most often what they learn through examples, like that of Robert E. Lee.

After the war, General Lee was walking in the snow on his farm when he heard his young son's crunching footsteps behind him. Turning, he watched the boy stretching to match his father's stride. Lee had this thought: "If my son is to follow me, I must make steps he can reach, and I must ensure that we are both going in the right direction."

That is the essence of Out Front Leadership!

Leading and Managing:
The Same or Different?

*You lead between paradigms —You manage
within paradigms.* —JOEL BARKER

A 1991 Leadership Studies International survey of 700 top corporate executives found 60 percent dissatisfied with their personal leadership efforts. Could these executives feel that their success was more a result of good management than leadership, and that stronger leadership skills would have produced even greater success? I would bet on it! This brings us to another critical question: Are the skills and traits of leadership the same as, or different from, those of management?

LEADERS VS. MANAGERS

Leaders may not have to *be* good managers; but when they are not, they had better *employ* good managers. Managers control today's business, while leaders transform the organization toward the future. Management is generally confined to less than 12 hours a day, while leadership is a 24-hour-a-day responsibility. Leaders dream, develop, and do; managers seldom dream.

As productivity follows creativity and form follows function, management follows leadership. Function is what you are responsible for doing; form is how you do it. Both leaders and managers have functions and forms, which are interdependent. The leader establishes and conveys the values and vision of the organization, and develops a master strategy to achieve the goals of that vision. The leader then empowers capable managers to develop and implement strategies for their departments that support the master strategy. As the managers organize, direct, and control their departmental strategies, the leader moves forward and beyond by innovating and by renewing the values and vision of the organization.

Management tones the body of the organization, while leadership is the soul—the pulling and driving force that enables each part to bring a meaningful contribution to the whole. As with a highly harmonized and highly disciplined professional athlete, the driving spirit balances and draws upon the interdependent powers of intelligence, size, strength, and speed, orchestrating the character of the whole (Figure 1). Success lies not in the domain of any single sphere, but in the interaction of all the spheres. From the center, the leader inspires and directs, more than controls, the independent and interdependent actions of the spheres.

ABOUT LEADERS

Before comparing or contrasting the skills and traits of leaders and managers, consider five of the major commonalities found in powerful leaders at all levels.

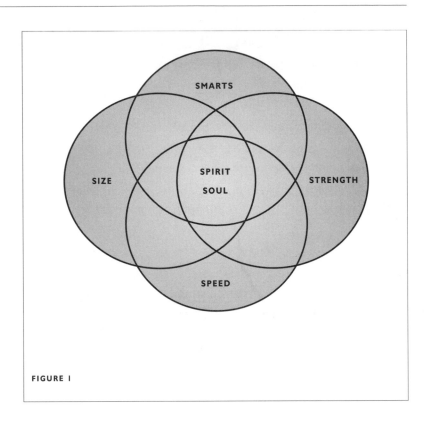

FIGURE I

- LEADERS FOCUS ON RESULTS.
  Leaders are more concerned with doing the right things than with doing things right. They are driven by desired results more than how the results are to be achieved.

- LEADERS BRING ORDER TO CHAOS.
  Leaders can deal with, and often thrive on, ambiguity. They simplify and moderate the chaos found between stability and instability.

- LEADERS OPTIMISTICALLY FOCUS ON THE FUTURE.
  Leaders believe that things can be better. They create new directions rather than maintaining the status quo. They shape culture by focusing on goals rather than obstacles.

31

■ LEADERS TAKE CALCULATED RISKS.
They make and act upon decisions based on facts, intuition, and faith.

■ LEADERS NURTURE EXCELLENCE.
Leaders consider their followers as the ultimate resource. They nurture self and others, seeking excellence, yet not demanding perfection. They ask no more of their followers than they demand of themselves.

Based on these common leadership qualities, Table 1 compares the skills and traits of leaders and managers.

In the comparison chart, I distinguished between the verbs "empower" and "delegate." Both actions bestow responsibility, but only empowerment gives the authority and accountability for final, "bottom-line" decisions. Both require competent recipients, but empowerment demands competence supported by conscience. The more a leader empowers people who are both competent and conscientious, the more power that leader has. Organizational crises arise when people without competence or conscience are empowered, or when the leader relinquishes authority for which he alone is accountable. Good leaders do not relinquish authority during crises, when followers need support, or when the unique expertise of the leader is required.

> *The most effective leaders, political or corporate, empower others to act—and grow—in support of a course that both leaders and followers find worthy.* —TOM PETERS

Being a leader does not imply abdicating the responsibility to manage. The leadership challenge is to be effective and efficient as both a leader and a manager. Leadership complements man-

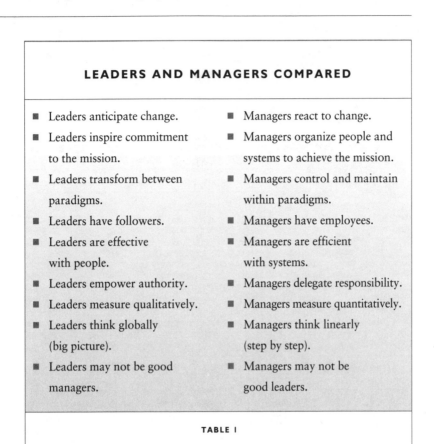

LEADERS AND MANAGERS COMPARED

■ Leaders anticipate change.	■ Managers react to change.
■ Leaders inspire commitment to the mission.	■ Managers organize people and systems to achieve the mission.
■ Leaders transform between paradigms.	■ Managers control and maintain within paradigms.
■ Leaders have followers.	■ Managers have employees.
■ Leaders are effective with people.	■ Managers are efficient with systems.
■ Leaders empower authority.	■ Managers delegate responsibility.
■ Leaders measure qualitatively.	■ Managers measure quantitatively.
■ Leaders think globally (big picture).	■ Managers think linearly (step by step).
■ Leaders may not be good managers.	■ Managers may not be good leaders.

TABLE I

agement; it builds, reinforces, and enhances management. Leadership is anticipating change and aligning people and structures to fulfill the mission. Management deals with the day-by-day, on-the-line achievement of the mission.

> *My horses seldom know that I am there—until they need me.* —WILLIE SHOEMAKER

33

The Leadership Choice:
Accepting the Challenge

*To be a leader means having (and seizing) the
opportunity to make a meaningful difference in
the lives of those who permit leaders to lead.*
—MAX DEPREE

In his 1954 book *Practice of Management*, Peter Drucker briefly recognizes the importance of leadership, but states, "Leadership cannot be taught or learned."

I vehemently disagree! Of course the egg and the sperm carry our genes, but they alone cannot make a leader. Leadership is not inherited but developed. It is taught by role models, and it is learned through practice.

✓ *Nurture is far more important than nature in determining who becomes a successful leader.*
—WARREN BENNIS AND BERT NANUS

THE LEADERSHIP CHOICE

To become a leader, we must choose to do so. We must unleash the power inherent in our freedom of choice, then channel that power to deliver.

We are known by the choices we make. Choosing to become a leader does not imply that we intend to become all things to all people. It means selecting a role in which you have the greatest potential for positive impact. This choice neither demands nor precludes seeking leadership at the highest levels. We need leaders at all levels to responsibly influence those above as well as below, and to unselfishly help others achieve their goals. A strong leader with five people who are committed to a common goal has more impact than a good manager with fifty people who merely report to him.

INFLUENCE VS. CONCERN

Wise leaders keep their areas of influence separate from their areas of concern. Stephen Covey, author of *Seven Habits of Highly Effective People*, defines our "concern circle" as including those areas or things we are concerned about but have no direct power to change as we do in our "influence circle" (Figure 2). Leaders are responsible in their circle of influence, but not in their circle of concern.

My experiences as a sales manager with Procter and Gamble can help explain these ideas.

- CIRCLE OF INFLUENCE.

    I was responsible for my personal performance, as well as the performance of those I supervised, in building our

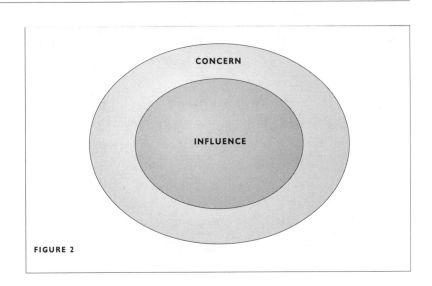

FIGURE 2

products' market share and profitability. Equally important, I was responsible for enhancing the P & G culture of continual skill training and company pride, and for training leader-managers for higher levels of responsibility.

- CIRCLE OF CONCERN.
  I was concerned with the effects of their job requirements upon the personal lives of those I supervised, as well as the effects of their personal lives upon their work. This included cases in which P & G provided outside professional counseling for drug abuse. Some employees chose a path to recovery, and continued to be highly productive. Others chose not to recover. When they made this choice, my responsibility for their performance put the situation back into my circle of influence, and I had to terminate their employment.

As leaders grow in skills and wisdom, they can extend their circle of influence; but it is irresponsible for them to do so when it is beyond their realms of competence and conscience. Leadership demands the understanding of personal limitations and the use of judgment in honoring Covey's Circles.

TAKING RISKS

To become a leader, we must also take the calculated risks required for discovery and growth. True discovery comes through seeing with virgin eyes, imagination, adversity, surprise, and risk. Many avoid taking risks because of self-doubt or fear of criticism.

> *It is not the critic who counts,*
> *not the one who points out how the*
> *strong stumbled,*
> *or where the doer of deeds could have*
> *done them better.*
> *The credit belongs to the man*
> *who is actually in the arena;*
> *whose face is marred by dust, sweat, tears,*
> *and blood;*
> *who strives valiantly;*
> *who knows the great enthusiasms,*
> *the great devotion;*
> *who spends himself in a worthy cause;*
> *who, at the best, knows in the end the triumph*
> *of great achievement;*
> *and who, at the worst, if he fails, at least fails*
> *while daring greatly.*
>
> —THEODORE ROOSEVELT

38

Calculated risk–taking is a strategic process. Following a "road map" much like the one used by Procter and Gamble in their decision to develop and market Attends, the geriatric diaper, can be helpful (Figure 3).

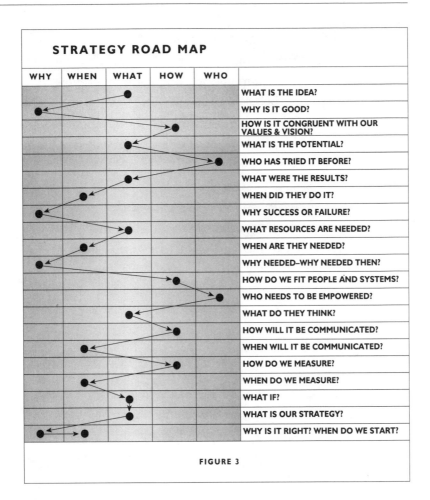

STRATEGY ROAD MAP

WHY	WHEN	WHAT	HOW	WHO	
		●			WHAT IS THE IDEA?
●					WHY IS IT GOOD?
			●		HOW IS IT CONGRUENT WITH OUR VALUES & VISION?
		●			WHAT IS THE POTENTIAL?
				●	WHO HAS TRIED IT BEFORE?
		●			WHAT WERE THE RESULTS?
	●				WHEN DID THEY DO IT?
●					WHY SUCCESS OR FAILURE?
		●			WHAT RESOURCES ARE NEEDED?
	●				WHEN ARE THEY NEEDED?
●					WHY NEEDED–WHY NEEDED THEN?
			●		HOW DO WE FIT PEOPLE AND SYSTEMS?
				●	WHO NEEDS TO BE EMPOWERED?
		●			WHAT DO THEY THINK?
			●		HOW WILL IT BE COMMUNICATED?
	●				WHEN WILL IT BE COMMUNICATED?
			●		HOW DO WE MEASURE?
	●				WHEN DO WE MEASURE?
		●			WHAT IF?
		●			WHAT IS OUR STRATEGY?
●		●			WHY IS IT RIGHT? WHEN DO WE START?

FIGURE 3

Incomplete data and the need for immediate action often preclude addressing all of the questions in this strategic roadmap, but it can still serve as a valuable checklist. A military leader in combat might consider no more than five of the questions. I doubt that Victor Kiam considered many more when, at the age of 52, he purchased the Remington Electric Shaver Company by persuading the Chase Manhattan Bank to loan him $40 for every dollar of his life savings. He paid off the debt eleven years ahead of schedule and doubled Remington's share of the electric shaver market in the process.

CHARACTER

Another element to consider in deciding to become a leader is character. Are you committed to continually improving your character? That is, being and doing better today than you did yesterday? Martin Luther, leader of the German Reformation in the 1500s, had a view of character that is equally valid today.

> *Good character is more to be praised than outstanding talent! Most talents are, to some extent, a gift. Good character, by contrast, is not given to us. We have to build it piece by piece through thought, choice, courage, and determination.*
>
> —MARTIN LUTHER

Good character includes the harmony of positive and productive habits, the repetitive behaviors that personify our thoughts, values, and attitudes. Productive habits of psychologically mature people are primarily self-nurturing processes, driven by focused discipline. This self-nurturing does not reduce the need for supportive reinforcement, but it serves as the core that guides our actions.

Mildred ("Babe") Didrikson Zaharias exhibited this maturity by setting the standard for female athletes and nurturing their efforts. She won two gold medals in the 1932 Olympics at 18, was an All-American basketball player, hit five home runs in one baseball game (acquiring the nickname "Babe" after Babe Ruth), and won five national golf titles—two after being operated on for cancer. She disqualified herself during a national golf tournament for hitting the wrong ball, even though no one else had seen the mistake. She established a trophy and financial support to be awarded annually to the outstanding woman athlete.

There are some men who lift the age they inhabit, till all men walk on higher ground in that lifetime. —MAXWELL ANDERSON

DEVELOPING YOUR LEADERSHIP

The Seven Characteristics of a Positive Leader

*We must try to keep ourselves in countenance
by examples of other truly strong people.*

—BENJAMIN FRANKLIN

Many admirable qualities are attributed to leaders—qualities such as emotional maturity, technical competence, devotion, judgment, empathy, vigor, and discipline. Positive leaders do possess these qualities, and more. I have found seven common characteristics that leaders share (I use the term "characteristic" because of the definitive value of its base, "character," and "common" because their commonalities are more powerful than their differences). These seven characteristics are integrity, compassion, cognizance, courage, commitment, confidence, and communication. They permeate the whole of a leader's, or an organization's, culture.

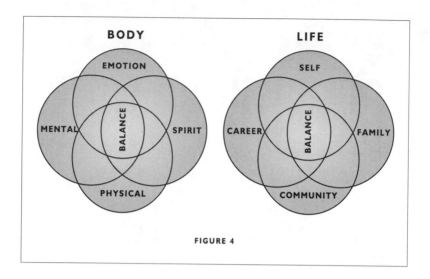

FIGURE 4

As there are four basic spheres of the body, there are four basic spheres in life (Figure 4). The interaction of the whole is more significant than the action of any of its parts. Changes within these interdependent spheres influence behavior within the parts, and the interactive productivity—the character—of the whole. Strict specialization in any one sphere upsets the balanced interaction of all the spheres. This necessary balance is like a woven basket in which each strand strengthens the whole.

> *Our sensations being very much fixed to the moment, we are apt to forget that more moments are to follow the first; and consequently, man should arrange his conduct so as to suit the whole—not just part—of life.* —BENJAMIN FRANKLIN

Part II, Developing Your Leadership, discusses each of the seven common leadership characteristics. You can develop them so that they permeate all the spheres of your life.

Integrity:
The Quest for Honesty

To thine own self be true;
and it must follow as the night the day,
thou canst not be false to any man.
—WILLIAM SHAKESPEARE

WHAT IS INTEGRITY?

Integrity is the unyielding battle for *what*, rather than *who*, is right. It is the seizing of responsibility, and the willing acceptance of the accountability that comes with it. Integrity is much more than not telling a lie; it is not living a lie! It is the removal of the many masks we wear to hide or deny our imperfections. The sign of integrity is behavior that demonstrates conscience and conviction, leaving little if any room for misinterpretation.

A CONTRAST

The daily price we pay for "fair dinkum"—Australian for "integrity"—is much less than what we pay later without it. To paraphrase TV ads for auto repair, "Pay me a little now, or a lot more later." The choices of two well known Americans illustrate both sides of this adage.

President Richard M. Nixon, re-elected to office with one of the greatest popular vote margins in American history, was informed that some of his campaign workers had burglarized the Democratic headquarters in the Watergate office complex. He was in no great danger of being personally implicated, but the actions of his staff were sure to cause embarrassment. Rather than uphold the law, to which he had sworn an oath, he attempted to protect his political image by ordering hush money paid to the miscreants. Because of his decision, Nixon paid a lot more later—and so did America.

In positive contrast was the unwavering integrity of Booker T. Washington. Born a slave and put to work in a coal mine at the age of nine, he rose from poverty and oppression to found the Tuskegee Institute. Washington was criticized by other black intellectuals, notably William E. DuBois, and ridiculed by many whites for his conviction that freedom is an earned responsibility. He was not referring solely to the recent slave status of African-Americans, but to the undereducated and undermotivated masses, black and white alike.

Washington defended this conviction when he addressed the Atlanta Exposition with his "Cast Down Your Bucket" speech in 1893. Can you visualize the public atmosphere that day? A 42-year-old black educator was speaking on the responsibility of freedom to a multitude that included many former slaves, unrepentant slaveowners, and unsympathetic public officials. The closest parallel I can think of would be someone defending capitalism in Moscow's Red Square in the days of Josef Stalin.

The integrity of leadership demands telling people what they need to hear, even when they don't want to hear it. A contemporary example is Joe Cannon's purchase of the Provo, Utah plant of U.S. Steel (USX) in 1987. After decades of union-management follies, USX was planning to close the plant and put 2,000 employees out of work. Union work rules had all but killed productivity; no one but an electrician was allowed to change a light bulb. CEO Joe Cannon told the union at Provo what they needed to hear: "We are your only hope—we do or die together." As a result, a contract was negotiated that reduced the workers' wage-benefit package from $24 per hour to $16 and shortened the contract from 272 pages to 46. A generous profit-sharing plan of $6,000 per worker offset some of the adjustment pain and helped change the corporate culture from compliance to pride.

> *Few men have virtue to withstand the highest bidder.*   —GEORGE WASHINGTON

6

Compassion:
The Responsible Attitude

*The art of leading, in operations large
or small, is the art of dealing with humanity,
of working diligently on behalf of men,
of being sympathetic with them, but equally,
of insisting that they make a square
facing toward their own problems.*

—S. L. A. MARSHALL

When asked to define compassion, people most often respond with the synonyms of benevolence, sympathy, commiseration, pity, fellow-feeling, or the "Golden Rule." For me, each of these falls short of a balanced and respectful linking between self and others. In the absence of balance between self-respect and respect for others, there is little understanding or unity. With this in mind, I have taken the liberty to expand upon the Golden Rule:

> *Do unto others, and yourself, as you would have others do unto you: be just in sharing, disciplining, and forgiving; stress positives, develop commonalities, appreciate uniqueness, be gracious in victory.*

EGO AND HUMILITY

This expansion is an often awkward combination of, and negotiation between, ego and humility—the self-assurance that you are good at what you do, counterbalanced by the outward recognition that, in many areas, there are others with stronger talents or skills than yours. Leaders capitalize upon their own strengths and align them with the strengths of others to achieve a common goal. In so doing, they develop productive alignments for the common good. They view the plural pronoun "we" as a mutually rewarding balance between "you and me." Would Sir Edmund Hillary have conquered Mount Everest if he had not supported, and been supported by, his Sherpa teammate, Tenzing Norgay?

Uncontrolled ego can become what mythologist Joseph Campbell called the "ultimate dragon." Adolph Hitler's uncontrolled ego led him to self-destruction, the fate of all supremacists. Charles Keating's debacle with America's savings and loan industry, while different in effect, was much the same in cause. Fragile and inadequate egos are also destructive; but, thank goodness, their spheres of influence and impact are significantly smaller. Add your perceptions of healthy and unhealthy egos to a few of mine:

SIGNS OF A HEALTHY EGO	SIGNS OF AN UNHEALTHY EGO
■ "We" attitude	■ "Me" attitude
■ Gives recognition	■ Demands recognition
■ Acknowledges mistakes	■ Blames others
■ Addresses opportunities	■ Emphasizes problems
■ Measures results	■ Measures excuses

CARING AND CONFRONTING

Compassion is the responsible and productive balance of individualism and teamwork. Sometimes it is "carefrontation"—the blending of caring and confronting. Confronting through principle supports caring, just as caring supports confrontation. As leaders care for the being and becoming of their followers, they also confront their detrimental behaviors and attitudes. This is far from being a new thought:

> *Do unto others as they need, or want, to be done unto.* —STUART ATKINS

> *Jesus comforted the afflicted, and afflicted the comfortable.* —UNKNOWN

Many parents and supervisors hesitate to discipline, thus harming their charges individually and collectively. Irving Siegel's findings, as reflected in his book *Parental Belief Systems*, imply that even some of the most responsible parents are tentative in their personal example of conduct and their disciplining of improper conduct by their children. Vince Lombardi, the late coach of the Green Bay Packers, was an avid supporter of carefrontation:

You can give me the greatest football players in the world; but if they won't practice the basics, if they refuse discipline, and if they don't care for each other as a close-knit family, I will not produce a winning team. —VINCE LOMBARDI

REWARDING ACHIEVEMENT

Good leadership includes searching for, and catching, people doing the right things as well as doing things right. It is *not* managing by exception. "Managing by exception" means followers never hear from their leader except when something goes wrong. Positive leadership means rewarding achievement as much as punishing misdeeds; but it does not exclude the latter when, in the leader's judgement, it is required. I have seen supervisors destroy the value and potential of employee performance reviews by focusing on negatives or emphasizing quantitative shortfalls over qualitative achievements. I have also seen supervisors refrain from candidly discussing incompetent performance with employees. Such supervisors, through their lack of objective compassion, inhibit performance and destroy potential.

Leadership compassion is helping others gain more authority and power in their responses to a more positive and productive life. The leader's role is not to do for others what they are capable of doing for themselves, but to continually develop capability and competence and to create environments in which each follower wants and accepts the responsibility and accountability for individual performance and behavior.

Cognizance: The Integration of Awareness and Knowledge

It is the learners who will affect the future. The learned find themselves equipped only to live in a world that no longer exists. —ERIC HOFFER

WHAT IS COGNIZANCE?

Cognizance is the power of knowledgeable perception that enables a person to use information effectively. It is the prevention of informational paucity as well as informational overload. It is an understanding of the past, an awareness of the present, and a vision of the future. Cognizance is continual discovery through seeing with new and searching eyes. It is the ability to understand and use ever-changing, complex, and ambiguous variables in the simplest and most productive way possible.

A leader does not allow an abundance of concrete facts to drive out intangible values. Viktor Frankl, the Austrian psychiatrist, was prisoner number 119,104 in Auschwitz and three other German concentration camps during World War II. Later, in his book *The Will to Meaning*, Dr. Frankl wrote—

> *Facts are not fate. What matters is the stance we take toward them.* —VIKTOR FRANKL

Leaders integrate the past with the present, then project it to forge a future. Frankl chose not to become the cynic who, in reliving the bitter lessons from the past, predicts disappointment for the future.

WINNOWING

Leaders develop the ability to separate the important from the unimportant, the relevant from the irrelevant. They find the meaning of events in history and understand that facts do not cease to exist when they are ignored.

Which was more important in the signing of the Magna Charta (a forerunner of the Constitution)—that it was drawn in 1215 by the English Assembly, led by the Knights of Shire, and forced upon King John? Or that it rejected the power of the king to control the personal liberty of the citizenry?

In *Mein Kampf*, Adolph Hitler clearly demonstrated his disdain for morality and the sanctity of human life, as well as his goal of global supremacy. His future adversaries looked, but did not see; listened, but did not hear—with the exception of Sir Winston Churchill. The English Parliament removed Churchill from office in 1935 for his cognizant but unpopular advocacy of preparing England for war with Germany. Guess whom England quickly awarded the role of Prime Minister upon the advent of war in 1940.

ADAPTING

The rules of guerrilla warfare were well established before our extended war in Vietnam: attack the enemy from unexpected directions, wear down his strength, outlast him, and fight for political as well as military advantage. Our leaders waged a positional, stationary war which played into the enemy's hands. We had the numbers on our side but we ignored the more important fact that the war of attrition was the enemy's war.

International industrial competition shares some of the attributes of guerrilla war—adapting to changing conditions and wearing down the opponent by hitting where he is weakest. The "Big 3" American auto manufacturers were either not aware of this similarity or chose to ignore it. They had lost 32 percent of the domestic auto market to Japan alone by 1987— almost one percent per year after Japan began exporting autos to the U.S. By 1984, the Big 3 had invested a combined $1 billion in R&D on a less-than-satisfactory safety airbag that would cost the auto purchaser $600 per vehicle. That same year, the Breed Corporation, a New Jersey explosive manufacturer, after only twelve months and $400,000 in R&D, developed a trigger that would reduce the airbag cost per vehicle to only $50. Each of the pompous Big 3 rejected Breed's product. Guess who did not? Toyota!

Apparently the facts that the devices worked well and cost less did not weigh as heavily as corporate pride. The Big 3, like many historically successful corporations, analyzed data and developed strategies through an "inside-out" procedure. With their size and resources, their "big is better" perception was "If we can't do it, no one can." They saw not the real environment but a nearsighted distortion of it. Toyota gained the advantage because they recognized the situation and acted astutely on the facts.

Digital Equipment Corporation was much like the Big 3. In 1977 its President, Ken Olsen, expressed the same noncognizant position when he stated, "There is no reason for any individual to have a computer in his home." I am certain his stance would have been different had he performed an "outside-in" analysis by surveying the market through his distributors and potential consumers.

KNOW YOURSELF—AND OTHERS

Cognizance goes beyond the awareness of history and the environments to the knowledge of cultures and the understanding of people.

> *He loses who knows not himself, his comrades,*
> *and his enemy.* —SUN TZU

How many of the following questions can you answer about yourself? Your spouse? Your teammates? Your corporation? Your competition?

- What is your goal or mission in life?
- Which persons or experiences influenced your choice of that goal?
- What boundaries have you established?
- What are your strengths and beliefs?
- Which skills do you need to develop?
- What is your current strategy?
- What sacrifices are you willing to make?
- What makes you unique?

This not-so-simple exercise gives rational direction to our behavior and future. However, if extended to hyper-reflection, it can unnecessarily delay or restrict action. When the centipede was asked by the toad which of its 100 legs it moved first, it paused to reflect and discovered it could not move at all.

*The real act of discovery consists not in finding
new lands, but in seeing with new eyes.*
—MARCEL PROUST

Winston Churchill saw with new and searching eyes. In 1942, three years before the end of World War II, he became confident of Allied victory and correctly shifted his focus to the potential of Russia's threat to future global peace. His awareness was heightened by his knowledge of Oliver Cromwell's major mistake when England was at war with Spain. Cromwell continued to consider Spain, although on the brink of defeat, as the only foe; in so doing, he ignored the impending threat of France. Churchill used the essentials of cognizance: he studied the past, and used the present to prepare for the future.

*Awareness is a key to successful human func-
tioning. It is difficult to reach our destination if
we do not know the territory.*   —WILL SCHUTZ

Courage:
The Backbone to Act

You gain strength, courage and confidence
by every experience in which you really
stop to look fear in the face.
—Eleanor Roosevelt

The fourth characteristic of leadership is courage—the courage to act upon your convictions with steadfast focus in the face of unrelenting opposition; the courage to sacrifice and risk, and not to take yourself too seriously; the courage to give, to enjoy, and to live! It is challenging adversity with grit and grace; and it is demonstrated by those hearty souls who move toward success, not away from failure.

PERSONAL COURAGE AND FEAR

We are face to face with our destiny and we must meet it with a high and resolute courage. For us is the life of action, of strenuous perfor- mance of duty; let us live in the harness, striving mightily; let us rather run the risk of wearing out than rusting out.

—THEODORE ROOSEVELT

Courage is not the absence of fear; it is recognizing and cop- ing with fear positively and responsibly. It is seeking challenges to overcome, rather than reacting to imposed challenges.

Courage is a self-developed skill that requires constant rein- forcement. I periodically competed in rodeo bull riding through age 54. It was not for the glory—for there was little glory in my "on and off before 8 seconds" record—but for the trial. The sweat of fear has its distinctive smell, and I know it well; but few actions cleanse and revitalize the spirit as well as facing the fear of risk.

It is courage, courage, courage that raises the blood of life to crimson splendor.

—GEORGE BERNARD SHAW

Psychological fear often takes a greater toll, and is more dif- ficult to overcome, than physical fear. Its most common form is the fear of failure. It may surprise you that this fear attacks peo- ple who succeed as well as people who fail. Those who were close to him feel that fear of failure caused the death of Karl Wallenda, the famous high-wire walker, who wavered and fell to his death while attempting to walk a cable between two 10- story buildings. Some might say Wallenda went beyond his limi- tations; yet he was still in his prime, and had accomplished similar feats before. I applaud Wallenda for facing his fear of failure, and for meeting death as he did life. The fear of death prevents people from living, not from dying!

I have known successful leaders who, unlike Wallenda, began hiding their fears and growing pessimism under the cloak of realism. These leaders had become successful by continually reaching challenging goals, but they began to set easier, "sure to win" ones, in effect retiring early from their careers as well as from the real joys of life. For the most part, these were talented people; but their talent was wasted for want of intestinal fortitude. Their fear of failure doomed their potential for continued success, and quite often that of their employees.

AUTOCRATIC COURAGE

General George Patton's leadership turned his soldiers from fear of failure to victory and glory. J. W. McLean, retired CEO of Banks of Mid-America, shares a personal anecdote about Patton. Shortly after the Battle of the Bulge in World War II, Patton held an intelligence briefing with all Third Army unit commanders and their staff. Patton told his commanders, "I want each of you to describe the condition of your unit, and what its needs will be as we move out to cross the Rhine in at least three places by April 20th. You have 90 seconds each."

The first commander made clear that his division was only 70 percent of normal strength, his ammunition supplies were only fair, and fuel for his tanks and trucks was only marginal. And so it went around the room in the minutes that followed.

Then Patton bellowed: "Now I'll give you just one minute each to go back around the room, and tell me how you mean to solve your so-called problems!" Patton's army crossed the Rhine on April 20th.

Patton's autocratic style is less suitable for peaceful and more democratic times, but it does make a valid point for lead-

61

ership in peace as well as war. Through personal courage and focused will, the leader disperses the herd instinct to withdraw in fear, and instills determination.

COUNSEL, INTUITION, AND FAITH

In the nonmilitaristic environment of the '90s, leaders develop courage in their followers more through cooperation and consensus than by command. They recognize fear as a sane human response to danger; they know that fears, like facts, don't go away when ignored. Leaders explain why action in the face of fear is important, what the calculated risks are, and how the risks could be even greater if no action were taken. They tell the reasons behind their decision, including their intuition and faith in the outcome.

In *Thriving on Chaos*, Tom Peters refers to courage in risk-taking as "intuitive judgement (supported with faith) in making good decisions based upon incomplete data." Intuition and faith are developed traits. Intuition is generally considered to be actionable knowledge without rational thought. I accept this definition, but not its limits. As described in Roy Rowan's *The Intuitive Manager*, I have enhanced my intuitive capability through a logical thought process. Rowan's Four Stages of Intuition Development are as follows:

1. PREPARATION
   - Visualize what you want—the end state.
   - Give yourself the freedom to conceptually create.
   - Understand the pulse of the environment (MBWA: "Management by Walking Around").
2. INCUBATION
   - Avoid agreeable thinking.
   - Avoid informational overload (analysis paralysis).
   - Avoid solving others' problems (MBWA: "Management by Walking Away").

3. ILLUMINATION
   - Rid yourself of preconceptions.
   - Be immersed in the situation.
   - Avoid rigid consistency.
4. VERIFICATION
   - Develop pertinent and qualitative support.
   - Periodically review data.
   - Listen to others' feedback. (Catalog hyphenated ideas—ideas of some merit by themselves, but of more merit when linked with others.)

Faith is a more personal trait. Faith is believing in someone, or something, greater than yourself; and through that believing, coming to see. It is through faith that I build my trust in my character, skills, and goals, and those of others, as well as our hopes for the future. Faith fills the void between the known and the unknown. It is the enduring conviction that the me I foresee is the me that I will be.

Yet, like all convictions, faith is futile without action:

> *Fear knocked,*
> *Faith answered;*
> *No one was there.* —UNKNOWN

GRIT AND GRACE

Margaret Thatcher led England for eleven years with the grit and grace of courage. Not only did she shatter the gender "glass ceiling" to become prime minister, she also held that position longer than any person in English history. Mrs. Thatcher strengthened England by her decisiveness and will, and by building consensus among influential parliamentarians of both parties. From the helm, she initiated major economic austerity measures, a firmer stance against the terrorist tactics of the Irish

Republican Army, and war to reclaim the Falkland Islands from Argentina. Like all responsible and productive leaders, Thatcher made mistakes; but this self-described "ordinary lady" led others to extraordinary standards. As England's prime minister, she personified the meaning of courage: responsible action toward a positive goal, supported by qualitative knowledge, intuition, and faith.

> *Life shrinks or expands in proportion to one's*
> *courage.* —ANAIS NIN

Commitment: The Passion to Fulfill Your Vision

I know by your deeds, that you are neither cold or hot. I wish you were either one or the other.
—REVELATIONS 3:15

One person with commitment has more power than a multitude who have only interest. The level of commitment is the key determinant. Some consider vision and mission to be the same, while others feel that vision precedes the mission. For simplicity, I use the terms interchangeably to mean a leader's overriding goal or ambition. I preface this chapter with my remarks on vision—for in the absence of vision, to what is a leader committed?

TO COMMIT OR NOT TO COMMIT

I'd rather be strongly wrong than weakly right.
—TALLULAH BANKHEAD

As a leader, your mission on earth is not finished as long as you are alive. In Richard Bach's *Jonathan Livingston Seagull* this theme epitomizes commitment. Yet I am continually amazed by the number of decent, well-educated, and highly regarded people who have no well-thought-through mission for what they want to accomplish and contribute. Those who have been successful without a mission could have been even more so with one. Unfortunately, the same holds true for many organizations and corporations. Many people in positions of respect have asked, "How do you develop a vision?" Without saying so, they are telling me that their level of contribution has been a result of their ability to react rather than to anticipate and plan. They choose to let their environment be the main influence in their lives. These people have no vivid picture of what they want, nor do they fully appreciate that real growth comes through creating and nourishing lasting value.

> *The smaller our mission, the less value we shall set upon it, and the more easily we shall be induced to give it up altogether.*
> —CARL VON CLAUSEWITZ

Growth in character and contribution blossoms only when leaders take on challenges larger than themselves.

DEVELOPING YOUR VISION

What are the basic steps in developing a vision?

1. Ask yourself: What is it that I choose to accomplish dur-

ing my life that will deliver the greatest contribution
to others, as well as myself?

2. Ensure that your vision is grounded in ethical values.

3. Include the elements of challenge, excellence,
   and clarity.

4. Word it in the present tense, as if it were an
   accomplished state.

5. Share it.

Each of these steps has been questioned in my seminars. Here are
the two most common questions, and my replies:

1. "Why must it contribute as much, or more, to others
   as to me?"

   REPLY: "Why is the cow more beloved than the sow? The
   cow provides sustenance to others while it is living."

2. "Why include excellence? If it isn't broke, don't fix it."

   REPLY: "In the era of Thomas Edison, people were
   satisfied with oil lamps."

COMMITMENT EXEMPLIFIED

Commitment to a vision is not a thornless rose; the rose is
growth, contribution, and reward; the thorn is sacrifice. Commitment means that the excellence of today is the expected of
tomorrow—the daily manifestation of the Kaizen Principle.

*An improvement of $1/_{10}$ of 1 percent in what you
achieve each day will result in a 27.1% improvement
over a 240-workday year.*

The Kaizen Principle of continuous improvement is like com-
pounding interest. As you can see from the example above,
building each day on the additive improvement of all the days
before yeilds more than the usual 24%.

Ignace Paderewski, the Polish concert pianist and states-man, demonstrated that commitment is not restricted to 240 eight-hour days per year. After one of his later concerts, a fan said to him, "Sir, I would give my life to play like you." Paderewski's reply: "I have."

Commitment is the concentration of will toward the fulfill-ment of your mission, and the self-discipline to do the hard work. True commitment does not know moderation.

> *The committed leader fears not extinction, but extinction with insignificance.*
>
> —ERNEST BECKER

Commitment is what drove Jimmy Yen to devote his life to teaching illiterate Chinese to read and write well into his eighties. Yen began his mission by teaching "coolies" (*kulai*, meaning "bitter strength") in France during World War I.

Commitment to significance was exemplified by Martin Luther King, Jr.—a commitment which, like that of Gandhi, led to his assassination. Dr. King, living his vision ("I Have a Dream") through sacrificial action, was largely responsible for America's laws on civil rights and voting rights.

BUILDING COMMITMENT IN OTHERS

> *Male or female, the effective leader wins com-mitment by setting an example of excellence: being ethical, open, empowering, and inspiring.*
>
> —JOHN NAISBITT AND PATRICIA ABURDENE

68

Getting others to commit to a common mission is one of a leader's most difficult challenges. You know when this challenge has been met in an organization by the individual and collective "pride of ownership." In a committed culture, you won't hear "I just work here" or "Sorry, I'm off the clock."

Leaders create commitment in others by agreement, not by force; through shared values and goals, they turn followers from selfish preoccupations to the pursuit of excellence. They ask no more from others than they are capable of giving—but more than they intended or thought possible to give.

Frances Hesselbein, Executive Director of Girl Scouts of America, is known for building commitment in the 50,000 volunteers of G.S.A. She says of her leadership, "I think I have kept my promises. I've been able to communicate a vision for the future, and my respect for people. We have a mission of excellence in everything we do. We are not managing for the sake of being great managers; we are leading and managing for the mission. We believe in helping people identify what they can do well, and releasing them to do it."

Confidence: The Belief in Yourself and Others

Not in the clamor of the crowded street,
Not in the shouts and plaudits of the throng,
But in ourselves, are triumph and defeat.
—HENRY WADSWORTH LONGFELLOW

onfidence is the steadfast reliance upon the values, beliefs, and competence of oneself and others. It includes, but is an extension of, courage. Confidence is cultivated by using our strengths and skills to extend ourselves and others a little further each day—taking that extra small step we doubted we could take, then one step more. Confidence is being guided by the stars, not by the lights of passing ships.

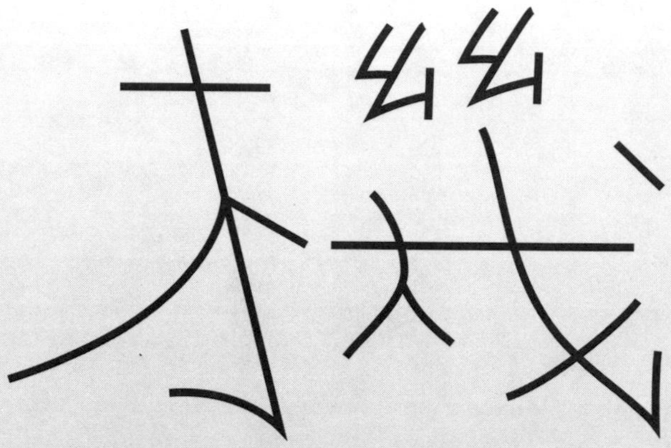

FIGURE 5

Good leaders know that a display of confidence can be inspirational. General "Chesty" Puller, one of America's most decorated combat commanders in Korea, when advised by his aide that the enemy had his Marine regiment surrounded, was said to have radioed his division commander: "We have been looking for the enemy for several days now. We've finally found them. We are surrounded. That simplifies the problem of getting to these people and killing them." Most of Puller's Marines came through the battle alive because of his confident example. General Puller later stated that his regiment's success in Korea was due to a unified belief in their mission and mutual reliance upon well-trained common and unique skills. I wonder if General Puller was aware that the Chinese character for "crisis" can also be interpreted as "danger," "important," or "opportunity" (Figure 5).

If you think you can, you can. And if you think you can't, you're right. —MARY KAY ASH

BUILDING CONFIDENCE

Leading is based on a belief in yourself, in the people you work with, in your profession, the future, and in the ability to achieve something more. —GEOFFREY M. BELLMAN

Confidence is built through successes and mistakes. It is developed by appropriate encouragement for the smallest steps of accomplishment, by praise for exceptional steps, and by discipline for errors—or inaction—in direct proportion to long-term consequences for established values and goals. A leader gives praise or discipline rapidly, radically, and without rancor or regard to position.

The greatest person is he who chooses the right with invincible resolution; resists the sorest temptations from within and without; is calmest in storms; and whose reliance on truth, virtue, and faith is most unfaltering. —W. E. CHANNING

What a brainload! Consider some of Channing's key words:
- CHOOSES.
  We have the power of freedom of choice. We can choose who we are today and who we will become tomorrow.
- RIGHT.
  What is right is more important than *who* is right.
- INVINCIBLE RESOLUTION.
  The courage of conviction persistently pressed forward by action, even when others see the cause as hopeless.
- RESISTS.
  The discipline of self-mastery to resist negative internal and external pressures.

- CALMEST.

  Positive in your strength and ability to influence the chaotic storms of change, thus enabling you to shape today for a brighter tomorrow.
- RELIANCE.

  Through adherence to common principles and values, you and your followers are mutually dependent and loyal.

CONFIDENCE IN CRISIS

Confidence is being prepared to fail, but not expecting to fail or accepting failure as a habitual condition. Everyone has setbacks, but leaders persist, and help others, to overcome them.

> *Never let the fear of striking out get in your way.*
> —BABE RUTH

Being prepared for failure builds confidence by providing a "best alternative" course of action. Professional negotiators employ best-alternative strategies to avoid impasse.

In his article "Surviving Crises," Paul Holmes suggested a four-point crisis prevention plan:

1. Anticipate possible crises.
2. Rank crises based upon potential significance of impact.
3. Develop contingency plans for each, with supporting resources.
4. Build good will before the crisis occurs.

This plan provides time and opportunity for study, preparation, and consensus.

But what do leaders do in a sudden, unexpected crisis, such as the poisoning of Johnson & Johnson's Tylenol? Situations like this required leaders to react strongly, of course. But the shock can be reduced through a contingency plan that can be adapted to the situation and implemented automatically when there is no time for discussion.

Elements of an all-purpose contingency plan can include the following:

- Determine the severity of the problem.
- Isolate the problem.
- Begin corrective action.
- Communicate to everyone concerned the situation, steps taken, and steps to be taken.
- Check progress and make necessary adjustments.
- Determine accountability.
- Communicate to everyone concerned the results and how to prevent recurrences.

I don't know if Johnson & Johnson had such a plan in place before their Tylenol crisis, but it certainly looks as though they did.

Confidence comes from running the gauntlet of adversities—like Helen Keller, who overcame unbelievable adversity in her journey toward excellence. Keller became blind, deaf, and mute at the age of nineteen months. With the assistance of her teacher and friend, Ann Sullivan, she learned to feel objects and associate them with words spelled out by finger signals on her hand. She progressed to Braille, and then to speaking, by feeling the positions of Ann's tongue and lips and mimicking them. Through slow and painful study and practice, Keller graduated from college cum laude at the age of 24. She went on to author ten books and to become an international counselor and lecturer for the American Federation for the Blind.

> *The world is moved not only by the mighty muscles of our heroes, but also by the aggregate of tiny repetitious shoves of each honest worker.*
>
> —HELEN KELLER

75

Communication:
The Power of Persuasion

Conversation is but carving!
Give no more to any guest
than he can digest.
Give him always of the prime,
and but a little at a time.
And that you may have your due,
let your neighbor carve for you.
—JONATHAN SWIFT

Confidence develops strong opinions, and leadership communications are predicated on those opinions. Leaders cannot afford to express their ideas through incomplete, mixed, or unclear signals in behavior or words.

As competence is ineffective without conscience, so are words without behavior. A good leader leads by example, supporting his or her behavior by verbal persuasion. To be effective, leadership language must be believed and responded to, and that is more difficult to achieve today than at any time in our history. Leaders must communicate needs, missions, trends, concepts, and quality-quantity linkages much faster, to more and better educated people and groups. They must shape their message for each audience, and set an example by acknowledging differences as well as commonalities. Most people respond emotionally to persuasion, then rationalize their opinion through intellect and/or belief. Thus, leaders must be both respected and believed in order to lead.

COMMUNICATION COMPONENTS

Few of us need reminding of the three components in persuasive communication (speeches, reports, etc.)—introduction, body, and closing—or that the body of the speech represents 85 to 90 percent of the total. However, from time to time many of us need to refresh our memory and practice the basic steps in preparing and delivering a speech.

MESSAGE. Tell them what they need to hear; support it with information, direction, and motivation. Sell them on the benefits of your ideas. This is very difficult when the leader must be the bearer of bad news:

> *It's a leader's job to bring the bad news, to get*
> *people to believe things they don't want to*
> *believe and then go out and do things they don't*
> *want to do.* —LEE IACOCCA

That is what the General Motors board of directors, under Chairman of the Executive Committee John Smale, had to do to initiate the drastic measures needed to save the corporation from bankruptcy and collapse. That is what President Harry Truman had to do when he removed General Douglas MacArthur from command of United Nations forces during the Korean War.

It is especially important in turbulent times for followers or employees to know and participate in success. Too often, leaders fail to acknowledge or celebrate achievement. The old adage, "When the going gets tough, the tough get going," can be grimly appropriate in unintended ways. When the "tough" do not feel leadership empathy in tough times, nor recall the pleasure and praise of success, they may soon "get going" elsewhere. In developing your message, be sure it is compassionate and in harmony with the occasion.

DELIVERY. The goal of delivery is to improve your relationship with your audience. Effective delivery requires sincerity, clarity, and a positive outlook. Clarity is the most difficult. The typical American dictionary contains more than 300,000 words, yet the average adult has a working vocabulary of fewer than 2,000. Of these, 500 are basic core words, such as I, you, go, do, yes. As Marlene Caroselli asks, which, then, is preferable, "scintillate, scintillate asteroid minific," or "twinkle, twinkle little star"?

NEGOTIATING

Negotiation skills are an important leadership communication requirement. I lay no claim to professional expertise in negotiating, but allow me to share some valuable lessons from being on the wrong side of the table from some very hard-nosed and capable negotiators:

1. Everything but integrity can be negotiated.
2. The best negotiators listen more than they talk, and they ask more questions than they answer.

79

Hear what a person wants to say, what he doesn't want to say, and what he is unable to say without help. —ELTON MAYO

3. Use restatement for clarification, restating what you hear the other parties say, using their words, tones, and body language.

4. Begin with commonalities, so that together you can constructively channel differences.

5. Recognize that there are very few pure win/win scenarios, but that all sides come out ahead when the negotiations are effective in reaching a wise agreement that meets objective standards, are efficient in using time and resources, and improve the relationships between the parties.

6. Recognize that there is always more than one issue: relationships are always an issue.

7. Replace "bottom line" demands with "best alternative" options. Balance power with conciliation.

8. Give the other party a choice between something and something else, not between something and nothing else. Build a bridge so the other party can gracefully retreat.

9. Use the power of "why," "what if," and "no"; but recognize "no" as a reaction, not an unchangeable position.

10. If you want a horse to jump a fence, don't raise the fence as it begins to jump.

11. Almost anything is easier to get into than out of.

12. Use the silence of a pause; the other party is likely to say more if you don't respond immediately.

13. Know who has the authority to make a decision.

14. Be serious about the purpose, but don't take yourself too seriously. Use appropriate humor to smooth rough edges, and to apologize when you are in error.
15. Share the credit and celebrate success.

> *Let us never negotiate out of fear. But let us never fear to negotiate.* —JOHN F. KENNEDY

PERSUASION

Leadership communication is the power of persuasion with authority. Communication, in all of its forms, is the vehicle through which leaders inspire others to reach higher with their hopes, their hearts, their minds, and their hands. Leaders recognize that communication marks the beginning of knowledge and the doorway to freedom.

Three of the most recognized and inspirational speeches in American history were Lincoln's Gettysburg Address, Kennedy's 1960 inaugural address, and Martin Luther King's "I Have a Dream." Less well known is the following by Harlee Branch, retired chairman of the board of the Southern Company:

"In this age of rapid and radical change, the creation and continuation of positive growth and good depends on our leaders; on their values, attitudes, and action more than just their skills. If they have purpose, confidence, concern for others, and real enthusiasm—their feelings more than just their words—they are bound to evoke a more favorable and positive thrust.

"In 1954, four million babies were born in America alone. These babies are now adults, with the vast majority having become a crowd. With this 1954 crowd and the ensuing waves behind it, we have substituted quantity for quality as a standard of measure; we have placed ourselves in the tyranny of the average, and we have educated many of our youth to emphasize process more than purpose.

"This crowd, this average, these process facilitators seek the easy way rather than the way of conscience and integrity. They are a people of the norm and, understandably, the unhappy. Contrary to what has been hoped, there is a tendency, even on the part of people with taste, talent, and honor, to apathetically accept the crudities of the average rather than renounce them and initiate higher standards of their own."

> *Not he is great who can alter matter, but he who can alter my state of mind.*
>
> —RALPH WALDO EMERSON

DELIVERING YOUR LEADERSHIP

Action for Contribution

*I find the great thing in this world
is not so much where we stand, as in what
direction we are moving. To reach the port
of heaven, we must sail sometimes with the
wind and sometimes against it—but we must
sail, and not drift, nor lie at anchor.*
—OLIVER WENDELL HOLMES

L eaders see themselves in the mainstream of life, the center of the world. From here they can see horizons, but no limits; they can influence, but not control; they can build consensus for excellence.

Part III of *Out Front Leadership* helps us avoid roadblocks to the rewards of leadership.

Roadblocks to
Becoming a Leader

We are our own jailer, and we have the key.
—O. G. MANDINO

The dictionary defines a paradigm as a model or template. Others have defined it more illustratively:

> *We see the world, not as it is, but as we are conditioned to see it.* —STEPHEN COVEY

> *A paradigm is a set of regulations that establishes boundaries and tells you how to behave within those boundaries.* —JOEL BARKER

An individual's or organization's paradigm is a self-chosen, self-developed, and self-perpetuated pattern of thought and behavior. It can be positive, as in the open-sided paradigm I earlier described to represent growth potential through the seven characteristics of leaders; or it can be negative, when totally enclosed by self-imposed restraints, barriers, or road-blocks. We are our own best friend or our own worst enemy. Ask a group of five-year-olds which of them can paint a pretty picture. They will all enthusiastically proclaim, "I can!" How would the same group respond 25 years later?

COMMON ROADBLOCKS

Too often, we set imaginary roadblocks for ourselves to make a seemingly comfortable prison of our lives:

> *They become as friends with their chains.*
>
> —LORD BYRON

When we do, our uniqueness and potential wither to insignificance. These chains, these roadblocks, feed off each other in a vicious circle, driving their confused victims toward a deteriorating status quo. It is self-fulfilling prophecy at its worst.

Five of the most common roadblocks are history, illiteracy, guilt, security, and apathy (Figure 6). In the center of this vicious circle is the black hole of self-defeat. Leaders help others avoid self-defeat by transforming roadblocks into open doors of opportunity and fulfillment.

HISTORY is the experience or knowledge of the past, even the past of only an hour ago. The past is to draw lessons from, not to live in. Lessons from the past must be considered in the light of their time; except for certain unchanging principles such as integrity and compassion, lessons from history must be adapted to the present. How often have we heard, "That's the way it is,"

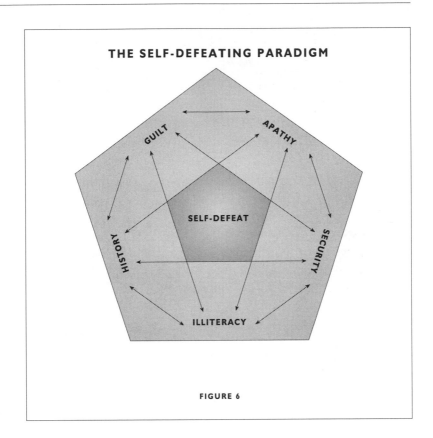

THE SELF-DEFEATING PARADIGM

GUILT

APATHY

SELF-DEFEAT

HISTORY

SECURITY

ILLITERACY

FIGURE 6

or "This has always worked in the past—why change?"? The past is to be acknowledged and understood, not clutched like a child's blanket.

Thirty years before his death in 1963, Aldous Huxley wrote:

> *Experience is not what happens to you. It is*
> *what you do with what happens to you.*
>
> —ALDOUS HUXLEY

This was written before diversity—gender, racial, or cultural—became a political and economic issue. What we did in the past, slotting diverse people ("them") into the prevailing culture ("ours"), will not work today.

The most important task at hand is to build from 100 cultures one culture, which no other culture has done before. Give a place to every human gift. —MARGARET MEAD

ILLITERACY is not confined to the 11 or 12 percent of American adults who are functionally illiterate. It includes those who do not develop new skills to replace obsolete ones, those who blame their status on lack of opportunity, those who search for excuses and blame others for their mistakes, and those who think they know it all. The first four can escape the illiteracy roadblock, but there is little hope for the last, whose unacknowledged illiteracy defeats them.

Alvin Toffler, the author of *Future Shock*, outlined a learning strategy for growth: learn how to learn, learn how to choose, and learn how to relate. Larry Wilson, founder of the Wilson Learning Corporation and the Pecos River Learning Institute, carries Toffler's "learn how to learn" even farther:

We cannot be satisfied just to respond, just to be reactive. We need to be able to leap ahead, to be creative and innovative, using "what if" to replace "that is the way things are." It means the gut-level understanding that old knowledge is the enemy of learning, and that [continual] learning is the key to creativity and growth.
—LARRY WILSON

Through learning, we have the opportunity to renew our becoming. We are works in progress.

GUILT has many nuances. Often associated with failure, it is experienced in many forms. When guilt cannot be removed, it must be accepted and transformed into something positive. It is a human choice to assume guilt, and it is a human being's responsibility to overcome it. There are times when we should bury our past; self-forgiveness, the conversion of guilt into positive experience, leads to self-healing.

A lesser, but more common, type of guilt roadblock is "guilt trip-itis"—allowing someone else to make us feel guilty merely for not acquiescing to their selfish desires. Followers often test leadership decisions through guilt trip-itis; good leaders do not accept this guilt.

SECURITY is not the absence of risk—it is the most foolish risk of all. In seeking security, we lose the opportunity for discovery and growth. Those who seek the comfort of stability become inflexible and resist change and innovation. Their need for equilibrium demands nonproductive control over the chaos of instability. Chaos will not be controlled or contained; it can only be used as an opportunity, the way a sailboat uses the wind.

Leaders are positive converters of the tension of chaos. Although leadership is put to its severest test in times of confusion and uncertainty, it also inspires and incites action from those who are immobilized by their security. The security of the status quo is not without tension; it is more negative, and less effective, than that realized through directed chaos.

APATHY, closely related to security, is the attitude that internalizes and magnifies negative stress. In today's environment, it is the most prevalent of all roadblocks. Seldom will its victims admit to it, even if they recognize it in themselves. However, it is readily apparent in those who think, "My vote doesn't count." Apathy debilitates the majority of adult Americans, who do not vote on issues or people, and those who say, "That's not my problem—let someone else handle it." Apathy thrives in those who vote for strict self-interest at the expense of justice and reality, or for representatives who tell them what they want, rather than what they need, to hear. It is found everywhere in our society, in those who are satisfied with mediocre performance.

Although the respected Russian author Aleksandr Solzhenit-syn is a dedicated, hard-line monarchist, he is often brilliant in his understanding of cultures and governments. In discussing the differences between the communist USSR and the USA, he said:

> *In the United States, the difficulties are not a dragon; not imprisonment, hard labor, death, harassment, and censorship, but cupidity, bore-dom, sloppiness, and indifference; not the acts of a mighty, all-pervading, repressive government, but the failure of a listless public to make use of the freedom that is its birthright.*
>
> —ALEKSANDR SOLZHENITSYN

The chains of self-defeat can be broken, but only if those in bondage are willing. Leaders support them in this effort, but cannot break the chains for them, nor command them to do so. With followers in bondage, leaders must sell, coach, and inspire.

Creating and Putting Your Vision to Work

If you have built castles in the air, your work
need not be lost; that is where they should be.
Now put the foundations under them.
—HENRY DAVID THOREAU

The future does not just happen, it is created! I agree
with Thoreau: it is action that makes dreams become reality. Dreams without action are little more than fantasies
or brain games.

As you enter positions of trust and power, dream
a little before you think. —TONI MORRISON

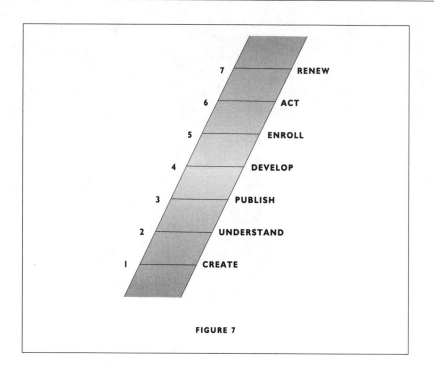

FIGURE 7

THE SEVEN STEPS

Vision development is like a ladder with seven rungs (Figure 7):

1. create your vision
2. understand current reality
3. publish your mission
4. develop your strategies
5. enroll others
6. act or perform, and
7. renew.

In preparing to take the first step—create—consider Marcel Proust's insight:

> *The real act of discovery lies not in finding new lands, but in seeing with new eyes.*
>
> —MARCEL PROUST

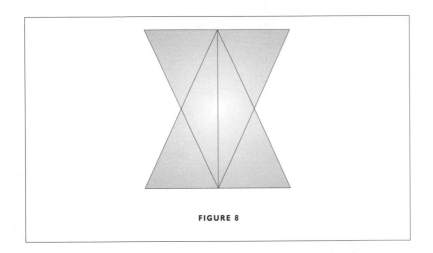

FIGURE 8

My definition is somewhat different: genuine discovery comes through unbridled imagination, seeing with virgin eyes, surprise, adversity, and risk. Separately, each of these results in discovery; combined, an even greater discovery. As with risk taking, imagination and perception are enhanced through continual learning and doing. What does your imagination allow you to see in the symbol that I use for leadership (Figure 8)? You may imagine you see 12 letters of the alphabet. If you did, was there communication or learning? You may imagine you see two hourglasses. If you did, did you perceive time? Can you define time? Is your definition different from mine: infinity to infinity, interspersed with measured or recorded events? What else do your imagination and perception enable you to see in the leadership symbol?

For a little imaginative and perceptive fun, connect these nine dots with no more than four connecting straight lines, and do so without removing your pen from the page (Figure 9). One solution is shown in Figure 10. Can you discover any others?

Perception is strong, and sight is weak.
—MIYAMOTO MUSASHI

95

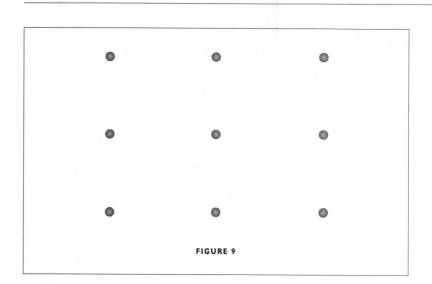

FIGURE 9

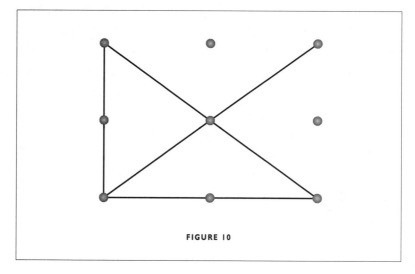

FIGURE 10

With a better appreciation for imagination and perception, let's see the rungs of the vision ladder through new eyes.

■ CREATE YOUR VISION.
Everyone should be committed to building something that he or she cares deeply about. Your vision might be part of

someone else's broader and more encompassing vision. My vision is but a small part of the overall vision of leadership, furthering responsible and productive freedom for the betterment of all humankind. During my previous career with Procter and Gamble, my vision was a compatible part of the corporate vision. A thoughtfully created vision is compatible with all the spheres of life.

> *It's got to be a vision you articulate clearly and forcefully on every occasion. You can't blow an uncertain trumpet.*
> —FATHER THEODORE HESBURGH

■ UNDERSTAND CURRENT REALITY.
Develop an understanding of the "macro" reality, the outside forces that affect your vision, and the "micro" reality, such as the knowledge and skills you have that will influence and be influenced by the macro forces. The macro is larger and more powerful than the micro. In corporate terms, the macro of an organization is more powerful than the micro of any of its employees—including the CEO.

The macro and the micro of your reality are much like the windowpane and the mirror. See through the pane for the skills and resources you need; look at the mirror to confirm those that you have. The macro reality of my vision is that our society needs more good leaders than ever before, and that leadership effectiveness is measured by public acceptance of the results. Unfortunately, public acknowledgement of value is often misplaced (e.g., the acclaim given to professional athletes who contribute only to their own glory) or limited to those with official titles (e.g., presidents, general, mayors).

Part of my vision is to broaden public acknowledgement of my success in developing leaders. This is where my "macro" meets my "micro." My micro reality is that I have led, and helped develop leaders, as a Marine, a construction supervisor, a sales manager, and a professional consultant. To fulfill my vision, I need to further enhance my communication and teaching skills.

- PUBLISH YOUR MISSION,

again and again. Without publication, there is little, if any, commitment; without repetition, it is soon forgotten. A mission espoused but not lived is hypocrisy. Members of Alcoholics Anonymous live with recovery through repetitive publication, and action in support, of their mission. I state my mission each morning, and at least part of it with each new introduction. Why have a mission you are not proud to share? My mission is this: I build leaders for the future! I help others discover, develop, and deliver their unique potential so that together we reach higher levels of excellence each day. I achieve this through "Out Front" example, and my teaching of the power inherent in our freedom of choice, positive growth principles, and behavior that displays those principles. I measure our collaborative results, qualitatively as well as quantitatively, through our contributions to society.

In my consulting, I have seen corporations without a written vision or mission statement, and others who had them, "somewhere." The latter are as negligent as the former. A few of their employees may recall having once seen it, without being able to recall what it said. For a mission statement to have meaning and clout, it must be published periodically to employees, customers, suppliers, and the community. This periodic publication should be reinforced by leaders at all levels during their business contacts, by emphasizing how progress toward established goals enhances the meaning and purpose of the vision. No situation is too insignificant to sell the benefits of the vision.

■ DEVELOP YOUR STRATEGY
with best alternatives for contingencies. Though principles and vision do not change, strategy must be flexible. Every mountain has more than one face to climb, and each face demands a different strategy.

Look at things [goals] objectively, from the viewpoint of the laws of the world; enact strategy broadly [flexibly], correctly, and openly.
—SHINMEN MUSASHI

Without strategy, your leadership and your organization will bounce from activity to activity, exhausting the strength of all resources. Without contingency plans, you lack the flexibility you need to take advantage of opportunity.

In deciding to write *Out Front Leadership*, I used a version of the decision strategy road map that I presented earlier (Figure 11). My strategy for this book is interdependent with other strategies (speeches, seminars, consulting, etc.) for my vision. It is important to know that each of my strategies is designed to make a profit. I need to profit to support my family, as well as to disseminate my vision.

■ ENROLL AND ALIGN OTHERS
with your vision, each according to his or her capabilities and needs. Without the commitment of others, there is no support for the vision. With your persuasion and help, others will commit, perform, and contribute to your vision.

99

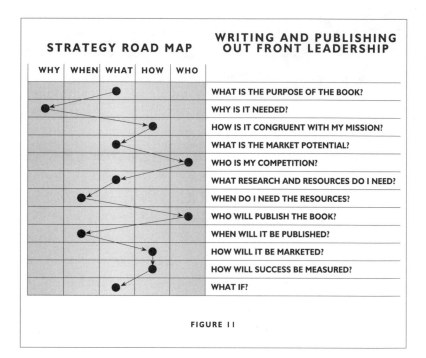

STRATEGY ROAD MAP					WRITING AND PUBLISHING OUT FRONT LEADERSHIP
WHY	WHEN	WHAT	HOW	WHO	
		●			WHAT IS THE PURPOSE OF THE BOOK?
●					WHY IS IT NEEDED?
			●		HOW IS IT CONGRUENT WITH MY MISSION?
		●			WHAT IS THE MARKET POTENTIAL?
				●	WHO IS MY COMPETITION?
			●		WHAT RESEARCH AND RESOURCES DO I NEED?
	●				WHEN DO I NEED THE RESOURCES?
				●	WHO WILL PUBLISH THE BOOK?
	●				WHEN WILL IT BE PUBLISHED?
			●		HOW WILL IT BE MARKETED?
			●		HOW WILL SUCCESS BE MEASURED?
		●			WHAT IF?

FIGURE 11

People do not enroll without understanding the benefits for themselves, as well as for something greater than themselves. Enrollment is the development of common interests and the channeling of differences for individual and collective fulfillment.

Leaders must enroll others in both purpose and performance, for purpose is powerless without performance. The time-tested leadership aphorism, "You are only as good as your followers make you," commands the leader to empower people who are both competent and conscientious, for leadership is a shared responsibility. Through this book, I seek your enrollment in my vision.

- ACT NOW!
  There are few perfect moments. Without action, you can forget the first five steps!

I certainly do not know everything about leadership; but if I were to wait until I do, I would never have completed this book or given leadership speeches and seminars. I would have failed to achieve any part of my vision.

- RENEW YOUR VISION
by continually reconfirming it. Leaders often overlook or ignore this step, taking it for granted. The leader and his empowered followers nurture each other by relearning and strengthening their relationships. This nurturing goes beyond the necessary reinforcement of principles, values, and vision. Renewal comes through risk, innovation, education, and the development of new skills in pursuit of excellence and fulfillment.

This book and my speeches and seminars are more a renewal and nurturing process than a creative one. Although in great demand, leadership and its development are nothing new; thus my effort is more to confirm than to enlighten. My enthusiasm for leadership is, in turn, renewed by the experiences and viewpoints of my audiences, and by my associates in various networks. As a result of this continual renewal, I am more excited about my vision and its potential than ever before!

CAREER MISSION

Quite often, young corporate managers ask if the seven-step ladder is applicable to their career mission to reach the executive suite. Yes, it is, with but a few changes in wording.

1. DEFINE your aspirations in terms of level of responsibility.
2. EVALUATE the skills you have and those you will need.
3. DISCUSS your aspirations with your supervisors and leaders.

101

4. **DEVELOP** your strategies and schedules.
5. **SOLICIT** support from your supervisors and associates.
6. **ACT** now!
7. **RENEW** through continual confirmation and nurturing.

For an additional boost up the ladder:

- Make contribution your goal, not prestige or power.
- Perform with excellence.
- When it is right to do—do it.
- Stand out while you fit in.
- Take some of the load off your boss's back.
- Seek assignments that others back away from.
- Do not assume that your supervisor appreciates your worth—show him, then show him again.

The higher you climb the corporate ladder, the more beautiful the rose—and the sharper the thorns! Which thorns are the sharpest?

- Professional loneliness.
- Loss of privacy.
- Conflicting expectations from different groups.
- Communication confusion.
- Dissent and disloyalty.
- Hectic schedules.
- More, and more complex, systemic relationships.

The shift in systemic relationships can be the sharpest of these thorns. One change can have a different impact on each person in a new and unstable environment. Each person or environment demands a different leadership style—that is, situational leadership.

Leadership Styles

The shoe that fits one person, pinches another;
there is no recipe for living that suits all cases.
—CARL JUNG

There is no single, all-encompassing leadership style that is best for all people in all situations. The most effective is whatever produces the best results toward a given goal in a given environment, with the people and time available. Leadership is the art of relating people, systems, environments, roles, time, learning, and change. The primary relationships are those of the leader with himself and with his followers.

PEOPLE RELATIONSHIP

The first relationship is the self relationship.

TODAY	SIX MONTHS HENCE	
_____	_____	**1.** I behave and speak in ways that demonstrate my values.
_____	_____	**2.** I adapt my style to the follower and the situation.
_____	_____	**3.** I give reasons for my requests.
_____	_____	**4.** I give my followers direction, resources, training, and reward or discipline commensurate with results.
_____	_____	**5.** I praise and criticize prudently, briefly, specifically, and as promptly as possible.
_____	_____	**6.** I pull others more than I push them.
_____	_____	**7.** I empower capable followers and give them the chance to lead.
_____	_____	**8.** I focus on long-range goals more than on short-term objectives.
_____	_____	**9.** I expect excellence, but not perfection.
_____	_____	**10.** I create environments that allow me and my followers to surpass personal expectations.
_____	_____	**TOTAL SCORE**

What lies behind and what lies beyond holds little significance when not compared to what lies within; it all begins with me! — UNKNOWN

Behind the second relationship lies the leader's recognition that, like him, each of his followers is a unique individual who desires, needs, and—in most instances—deserves respect.

Through relationships we develop our leadership habits. The preceding exercise will give you an indication of your own habits. Use only five numbers in responding to each question: *5 = always, 4 = often, 3 = half the time, 2 = seldom, 1 = never.* Wait six months before completing the second column; then you can measure and celebrate your growth.

Don't be disheartened by your score. I know of no one who has scored anywhere close to 50. No average or median score has been developed for this self-appraisal, nor should there be. The test is simply a vehicle to provide direction for leadership growth. Based on your responses, what practices will you continue? Start doing? Stop doing?

FOLLOWER READINESS

In 1985, the Center for Leadership Studies identified four levels of follower performance readiness. These levels and their corresponding needs for direct leadership participation are shown in Table 2. There is a basic leadership style to meet each of the four leadership needs of the followers. None is perfect for all objectives in all

FOLLOWER READINESS	LEADERSHIP NEED
LEVEL 1 ABLE, WILLING, AND CONFIDENT	LOW DEMOCRATIC (D)
LEVEL 2 ABLE, BUT UNWILLING, OR INSECURE	MEDIUM–LOW DEMOCRATIC AUTOCRACY (DA)
LEVEL 3 UNABLE, BUT WILLING, OR CONFIDENT	MEDIUM–HIGH AUTOCRATIC DEMOCRACY (AD)
LEVEL 4 UNABLE, AND UNWILLING, OR INSECURE	HIGH AUTOCRATIC (A)

TABLE 2

LEADERSHIP STYLES

SOURCE	DEMOCRATIC (D)	DEMOCRATIC AUTOCRACY (DA)	AUTOCRATIC DEMOCRACY (AD)	AUTOCRATIC (A)
CENTER FOR LEADERSHIP STUDIES	PERSONAL POWER PEOPLE DRIVEN	PERSONAL/ POSITION POWER PEOPLE/TASK TASK DRIVEN DELEGATES CONTROLS	POSITION/ PERSONAL POWER TASK/PEOPLE DRIVEN CONTROLS/ DELEGATES	POSITION POWER TASK DRIVEN CONTROLS
LARRY WILSON "CHANGING THE GAME"	INNOVATION PARTNERING VALUE ADDED	PROBLEM SOLVING COOPERATIVE INDEPENDENCE TACTICAL		PARADIGMATIC COMPETITIVE SURVIVAL
ROY ROWAN "INTUITIVE MANAGER"	PROACTIVE SPHERICAL LONG TERM			REACTIVE LINEAR SHORT TERM
LAWRENCE MILLER "BARBARIANS TO BUREAUCRATS"	SYNERGIST	EXPLORER	BUILDER	BARBARIAN
BENNIS & NANUS "LEADERS"	TRANSFORMS SYMBIOTIC PRIDE CULTURE			CAUSE & EFFECT FEAR COMPLIANCE CULTURE
KENNETH BLANCHARD "LEADERSHIP AND THE ONE-MINUTE MANAGER"	EMPOWERING	SUPPORTING	COACHING	DIRECTING

TABLE 3

environments. As follower readiness changes, the necessary leadership style also changes. By tailoring leadership style and level of involvement to the situation, the leader coaches the followers' performance and mentors their development.

LEADERSHIP STYLES

Leadership is strategically situational.—KENNETH BLANCHARD

Many leadership experts view the four basic leadership styles similarly, but describe them differently (Table 3).

PERSONAL ORIENTATION				
	SUPPORTING/ GIVING	**CONTROLLING/ TAKING**	**CONSERVING/ HOLDING**	**ADAPTING/ DEALING**
GOALS	PROVE WORTH BE HELPFUL	BE COMPETENT GET RESULTS	GO SLOW BE SURE	KNOW PEOPLE GET ALONG
OUTER ACTIONS	PRINCIPLED— COOPERATIVE	PERSISTENT— INITIATING	SYSTEMATIC— ANALYTICAL	HARMONIUS— TACTFUL
	DEDICATED— PURSUES EXCELLENCE	URGING— DIRECTING	MAINTAINING— TENACIOUS	FLEXIBLE— AWARE
STRENGTH STATEMENTS	MUST FEEL WORK IS RELEVANT	QUICK TO SEIZE OPPORTUNITY	METHODICALLY FOLLOWS PROCEDURES	USES PERSONAL CHARM
	WANTS TO BENEFIT PEOPLE	LIKES VARIETY	RELIES HEAVILY ON ANALYSIS AND LOGIC	SENSITIVE TO OTHERS
	DEFENDS OTHERS' RIGHTS	ENJOYS CHALLENGE OF DIFFICULT	USES TRADE-OFFS IN OPTIONS	FITS IN WITH ALL PEOPLE
	WANTS TO DETERMINE DIRECTION	LIKES TO BE IN CONTROL	LIKES TO USE TRIED & TRUE	QUICK TO ADAPT
STRENGTH ADJECTIVES	THOUGHTFUL— IDEALISTIC	COMPETITIVE— FORCEFUL	TENACIOUS— PRACTICAL	FLEXIBLE— TACTFUL
	TRUSTING— COOPERATIVE	SELF-CONFIDENT— URGENT	ECONOMICAL— ANALYTICAL	SOCIAL— YOUTHFUL
	HELPFUL— RECEPTIVE	DIRECTING— PERSISTENT	RESERVED— STEADFAST	ENTHUSIASTIC— INSPIRING
	RESPONSIVE— LOYAL	SEEKS CHANGE— RISK TAKER	FACTUAL— THOROUGH	EXPERIMENTAL— ANIMATED
	SEEKS EXCELLENCE	PERSUASIVE	METHODICAL	NEGOTIATING
MESSAGES/ METHODS OF MOTIVATION	SHOW THAT THE IDEA IS THE RIGHT THING TO DO AND GOOD FOR ALL CONCERNED.	INDICATE CHALLENGES INVOLVED AND OPPORTUNITIES FOR ACTION AND PAY OFF.	PRESENT IDEA LOGICALLY IN A FACTUAL MANNER.	SOCIALIZE BEFORE PRESSING FOR DECISION & SHOW WILLINGNESS TO COMPROMISE.
	SHOW THAT IDEA IS CONSISTENT WITH PRINCIPLES AND STANDARDS OF EXCELLENCE.	INDICATE THE EXTENT TO WHICH THEY WILL BE IN CHARGE.	USE THE FAMILIAR—TYING NEW THINGS TO OLD. SHOW LOW RISK INVOLVEMENT.	SHOW THAT THE IDEA MEETS THE APPROVAL OF THE MAJORITY OF THE PEOPLE INVOLVED.
	STRESS FAIRNESS AND HELPFULNESS OF THE IDEA. INDICATE YOUR NEED(S).	STATE THE IDEA DIRECTLY WITH CONFIDENCE AND ENTHUSIASM.	DOCUMENT HOW THE IDEA WORKED IN THE PAST AND THAT ACTION IS NEEDED TO PRESERVE WHAT THEY ALREADY HAVE.	USE LIGHT APPROACH BEING AS INFORMATIVE AS POSSIBLE.

TABLE 4

107

STUART ATKINS

The effectiveness of any leadership style is enhanced by considering the followers' personal orientations (Table 4). This relationship-building guide, developed by Stuart Atkins and the Human Resources Technology Company, promotes a more cohesive and productive collaboration between leader and followers. As with leadership style, no single orientation is perfect or best, and we each have one or more of the attributes shown in each of the four orientations. We also each have a primary and a secondary orientation. With very few people is one orientation overwhelmingly predominant.

Our orientations do influence our leadership styles, but there is little other correlation between the two. For example, a leader with a supporting/giving orientation is capable of effectively using any of the leadership styles. I have improved and enhanced the effectiveness of my leadership style with followers at all levels of readiness by applying these principles.

Had I learned the lessons of style and orientation earlier, I would not have made some of the mistakes that I did. For example and your benefit, I share one of my "people" mistakes. As a field sales manager, I promoted a sales representative, whom I will call Stan, to first-level manager because of his history of exceptional sales results. Stan did well as a manager for a while by establishing "good old boy" relationships with his customers and salespeople. His short-term success was a result of his adapting/dealing personal orientation and his consistently democratic leadership style—regardless of follower readiness or situation. As job demands became more challenging and the interdependent systems more complex, Stan and several of his sales reps became less capable and less confident in their performance. They became willing level fours in terms of follower readiness (willing, but unable and insecure).

Stan was an avid competitor, which I misinterpreted as a personal orientation identical with my primary one—controlling/taking. I compounded this error through my almost constant use of the

NEEDS	A. MASLOW TERMS	CORPORATE TERMS
PHYSICAL	WATER, FOOD, SHELTER, CLOTHING, FREEDOM	WAGES, INSURANCE, BENEFITS
SECURITY	SAFETY, STABILITY, PREDICTABILITY	WORK CONDITIONS, VALUES, SENIORITY, PENSION
SOCIAL	LOVING, BEING NEEDED, BELONGING	SUPPORT, OPENNESS, TEAM SPIRIT
EGO	SELF ESTEEM, PRESTIGE	ACHIEVEMENT, SKILLS DEVELOPMENT, RECOGNITION
SELF-ACTUALIZATION	PERSONAL GROWTH, CREATIVITY, CONTRIBUTION	INNOVATION, AUTHORITY, AUTONOMY

TABLE 5

autocratic leadership style. Through short-term tasks, measures, and survival motivation, I pushed Stan into the ineffective "cover your ass" mode of behavior. As you would guess, Stan became less able, lost confidence, and soon left the corporation. I learned a big lesson, but at the expense of Stan and my employer.

FOLLOWER NEEDS

All people have needs for pride, dignity, and respect, as well as others that the leader must help them to realize. Abraham Maslow identified several of these needs, which Table 5 translates into corporate terminology.

As the fulfillment of a follower's needs ascends towards self-actualization, his need for direct leadership decreases; the follower becomes a self-leader.

Leaders often mistakenly assume that they know what is important to a follower. What employers consider most important to employees is often quite different from the employees' priorities. This is shown in a survey conducted by Professor Ken Kovac at the University of Maryland (Table 6).

HOW EMPLOYEES AND EMPLOYERS RANK JOB FACTORS		
IMPORTANCE TO EMPLOYEE	RANKING AREA	IMPORTANCE TO EMPLOYER
1	Employee appreciation	8
2	Being considered an insider	10
3	Personal sympathy	9
4	Job security	2
5	Wages	1
6	Interesting work	5
7	Promotions	3
8	Loyalty	6
9	Work conditions	4
10	Tactful discipline	7

TABLE 6

KEN KOVAC

It is interesting that the employees' top three were ranked by the employers in the bottom three. The employers in this survey were not managing by walking around, nor were they asking the right questions of the right people.

COMMON ERRORS

Failing to ask the right questions is but one of many mistakes that can diminish or destroy leadership effectiveness. Other common mistakes are these:

- Unharnessed manipulation of others. Manipulation can be effective, even necessary, in times of crisis or when dissent or disloyalty by a few is detrimental to the many, but is destructive when used routinely.
- Inconsistency of purpose, which results in loss of focus.
- Measuring quantity without measuring quality.
- Failure to anticipate crises.
- Demanding short-term results that hinder or defeat the success of long-term goals.

- Getting comfortable, or allowing others to get comfortable, in a job or role.
- Failure to understand the importance of profit.
- Becoming trapped in routine.
- Instituting systems that generate more paper than they replace.
- Allowing followers to become so dependent that they "put their monkey on your back."
- Developing an "us versus them" attitude, other than with external competition.
- Failure to develop or understand the necessary linkages between interdependent systems.
- Attacking the person, rather than attacking wrong behavior by the person.
- Thinking you are responsible *for* someone more than being responsible *to* them.
- Being a "good old boy"—striving to be liked more than respected.
- Failure to use time effectively. What are you getting in return for the 86,400 seconds you invest each day?
- Unawareness of hidden reasons why followers fail to perform.

F. F. Fournies addresses this last, common mistake in his book *Why Employees Don't Do What They Are Supposed to Do.* Some of his conclusions are these:

- They think they are doing it.
- They don't know why they should do it.
- They don't know what they are supposed to do; or how, or when.
- They think something else is more important.
- They think your way will not work.
- There is no positive consequence to them for doing it.

- They are rewarded for not doing it.
- There are consequences beyond their control.

Leaders, like all people, are imperfect. Everyone makes mistakes. The difference is that good leaders learn through, benefit from, and are accountable for their mistakes, and they seldom make the same mistake twice. Those who don't make mistakes are surviving, not living; retreating, not attacking!

LEADERSHIP PRINCIPLES

Although I know that my military training has been invaluable in the development of my leadership styles, I don't consider it a prerequisite. The time-tested leadership principles that I learned in the Marine Corps can be used by leaders in any environment. Consider a few of the following in developing your leadership styles:

- Get out front of your followers, except when it comes to water, food, and shelter.
- Recognize that the mission comes first. This may require the undesired sacrifice of some good and capable people.
- Instill and perpetuate the will to endure and achieve. This level of will delivers far beyond the limits of physical stamina.
- Strategies are flexible; principles and purpose are not.
- The leader's attitude is manifested in the followers'.
- Train the followers in conditions as close to real as possible.
- Disperse the herd instinct of fear and negativism.
- Leaders have problem followers and followers with problems. Give discipline to the former, and understanding to the latter; but do not assume the role of God!
- Do not retire the strong or allow the inept to teach.
- Appreciate the differences in demand between initiating

and implementing a command. Initiate only what you are committed to follow through on.

- Train your people to think unconventionally.
- Loyalty is not given upward, when not received downward.

Expect excellence. Whichever leadership styles or principles you use, execute them to inspire excellence in conduct and contribution.

> *The quickest way to kill human spirit is to ask someone to do mediocre work.* —AYN RAND

Even the most capable people will become less capable in a stagnant and unchallenging environment, regardless of your leadership style. Good leaders give followers opportunities to learn and perform beyond their expectations.

15

Developing and Transforming the Organization

*People in authority must be social architects, study-
ing and shaping what we call the "culture of work";
examining the values and norms of organizations,
and the ways they are transmitted to the individual;
and, where necessary, altering them.*

—WARREN BENNIS

very year more small businesses start up and fail, and more
big businesses restructure or downsize. Whether small
or large, businesses either become stronger or fail—they
cannot stand still and survive. When a business prospers, it
is leaders at all levels that make it work. What is it that these
successful business leaders do?

1. They avert disaster, then seize the initiative.
2. They create, renew, and communicate a future-driven mission of excellence.
3. They develop a culture based on steadfast principles and values.
4. They strengthen internal structures for maximum external impact.
5. They plan for leadership succession.

This chapter addresses points three and four; the first two were discussed previously, and the fifth will be discussed in the final chapter.

STATEMENT OF PURPOSE

Organizational culture begins with and is enhanced and renewed by leadership behavior that fits the organization's published vision and statement of purpose. It may surprise you to learn that many organizations have neither of these in place. If nothing else, an organization should have a statement of purpose as simple and generic as this:

> *We are committed to excellence. We deliver,*
> *beyond expectations, upon both our short-term*
> *and long-term commitments to all customers.*
> *We measure our results by growth in quality*
> *(products, service, relationships, environments,*
> *and innovations) as well as quantity*
> *(sales, profits, and market share.)*

I understand that Jack Welch, CEO of the General Electric Corporation, has a statement of purpose for his organization that is even simpler: "Service through speed, simplicity, and self-confidence."

CULTURAL PRINCIPLES

Cultures are established by firm and consistent leadership conduct: behavior based on unchanging values and principles, providing security for performance and growth, but flexible enough to meet unexpected challenges. By observing and questioning several organizations, I developed the following list of cultural principles that are conducive to a positive growth environment:

1. We do not negotiate our integrity, nor do we violate ethical or legal codes of conduct.

2. We constantly strive for excellence, measured in terms of quality as well as quantity.

3. We innovate, anticipate change, and take calculated risks.

4. We build mutually productive long-term alliances with all customers through the Value Equation:

$$\text{VALUE} = \frac{\text{BENEFITS} - \text{DISSATISFIERS}}{\text{COST}}$$

5. We employ exceptional people, clearly defining performance expectations and levels of authority. Our employees are recognized commensurate with their contribution and are given the chance to realize their potential.

6. We operate lean, not allowing necessary variable costs to become unnecessary fixed costs. Our employees understand profits and costs, and accept personal responsibility for both.

7. We commit resources based on performance and potential. We do not develop new businesses to the detriment of our established profitable business.

8. We are a valued asset to our communities and environments.

9. We value a positive, "work is fun" approach to productivity.

TRANSFORMING STRUCTURES

With these cultural principles as a foundation, leaders continually adapt the organization's structure for maximum external effectiveness. They recognize that there is no single, sacred structure that can guarantee growth and productivity. As the environment changes, or as the leaders believe it will change, current structures may need renovation or replacement. Total restructuring is usually unnecessary in organizations that continually adapt. The major factors influencing organizational structures are the mission, current and future environments, and resources (people, money, time, systems, etc.).

There are three basic organizational structures (and many hybrids), each hierarchical in design. A startup organization generally begins as a monarchy and, as it grows, evolves into an oligarchy or a democracy. The following are simplified diagrams of the three basic structures (Figure 12).

Whatever the structure, its purpose is to provide a framework through which the organization can fulfill its mission most effectively, efficiently, and cooperatively.

PHILOSOPHICAL CONSIDERATIONS

In designing and developing structures, there are certain philosophical considerations:

- Strong leadership at lower levels strengthens leadership at top levels, when the top levels don't fear loss of power or prestige.
- Leadership dispersion ranks second only to the Rule of Law as a means of domesticating power and ensuring liberty. (John Gardner, *On Leadership*)
- The need for hierarchical leadership is fundamental to man. (Antony Jay, *Management and Machiavelli*)
- You need to reward people by the contribution they make, not by level or status. (Rosabeth Moss Kanter, *The Challenge of Organizational Change*)

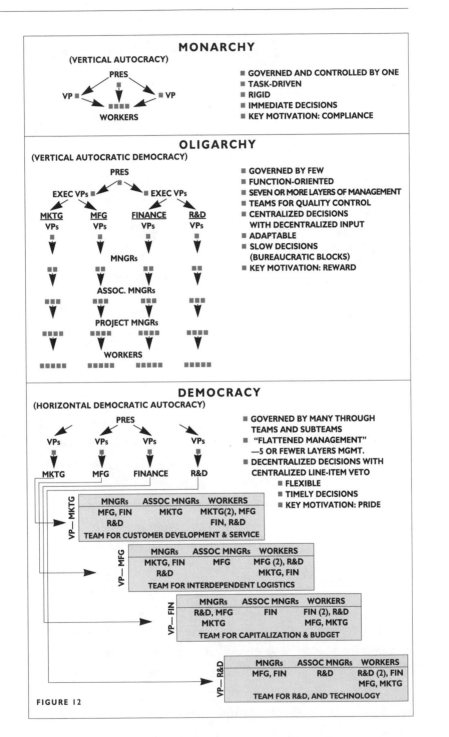

MONARCHY

(VERTICAL AUTOCRACY)

PRES

VP ◼ ◼ VP

WORKERS

- GOVERNED AND CONTROLLED BY ONE
- TASK-DRIVEN
- RIGID
- IMMEDIATE DECISIONS
- KEY MOTIVATION: COMPLIANCE

OLIGARCHY

(VERTICAL AUTOCRATIC DEMOCRACY)

PRES

EXEC VPs ◼ ◼ EXEC VPs

MKTG MFG FINANCE R&D
VPs VPs VPs VPs

MNGRs

ASSOC. MNGRs

PROJECT MNGRs

WORKERS

- GOVERNED BY FEW
- FUNCTION-ORIENTED
- SEVEN OR MORE LAYERS OF MANAGEMENT
- TEAMS FOR QUALITY CONTROL
- CENTRALIZED DECISIONS
  WITH DECENTRALIZED INPUT
- ADAPTABLE
- SLOW DECISIONS
  (BUREAUCRATIC BLOCKS)
- KEY MOTIVATION: REWARD

DEMOCRACY

(HORIZONTAL DEMOCRATIC AUTOCRACY)

PRES

VPs VPs VPs VPs

MKTG MFG FINANCE R&D

- GOVERNED BY MANY THROUGH
  TEAMS AND SUBTEAMS
- "FLATTENED MANAGEMENT"
  —5 OR FEWER LAYERS MGMT.
- DECENTRALIZED DECISIONS WITH
  CENTRALIZED LINE-ITEM VETO
  - FLEXIBLE
  - TIMELY DECISIONS
  - KEY MOTIVATION: PRIDE

VP— MKTG

MNGRs	ASSOC MNGRs	WORKERS
MFG, FIN	MKTG	MKTG(2), MFG
R&D		FIN, R&D

TEAM FOR CUSTOMER DEVELOPMENT & SERVICE

VP— MFG

MNGRs	ASSOC MNGRs	WORKERS
MKTG, FIN	MFG	MFG (2), R&D
R&D		MKTG, FIN

TEAM FOR INTERDEPENDENT LOGISTICS

VP— FIN

MNGRs	ASSOC MNGRs	WORKERS
R&D, MFG	FIN	FIN (2), R&D
MKTG		MFG, MKTG

TEAM FOR CAPITALIZATION & BUDGET

VP— R&D

MNGRs	ASSOC MNGRs	WORKERS
MFG, FIN	R&D	R&D (2), FIN
		MFG, MKTG

TEAM FOR R&D, AND TECHNOLOGY

FIGURE 12

119

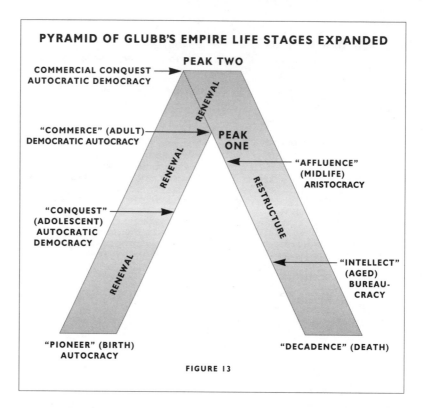

PYRAMID OF GLUBB'S EMPIRE LIFE STAGES EXPANDED

PEAK TWO

COMMERCIAL CONQUEST
AUTOCRATIC DEMOCRACY

RENEWAL

"COMMERCE" (ADULT)
DEMOCRATIC AUTOCRACY

PEAK
ONE

RENEWAL

"AFFLUENCE"
(MIDLIFE)
ARISTOCRACY

RESTRUCTURE

"CONQUEST"
(ADOLESCENT)
AUTOCRATIC
DEMOCRACY

RENEWAL

"INTELLECT"
(AGED)
BUREAU-
CRACY

"PIONEER" (BIRTH)
AUTOCRACY

"DECADENCE" (DEATH)

FIGURE 13

- Decentralization does not produce decision autonomy when procedures and rules are increased to ensure that order reigns, and when adequate resources are not provided. (Abraham Zaleznik, *Managerial Mystique*)
- Democracy was conceived as a combination of liberty and the assumption of responsibility. (W. W. Rostow, *Politics and Stages of Growth*).

ORGANIZATION LIFE CYCLE

Much of the corporate restructuring we see today would have been unnecessary had those corporations renovated their house as it aged. Without continual adaptation, restructuring is inevitable. Often, it is too late to prevent permanent damage or demise; the average Fortune 500 corporation stays on the list only 35 years.

In his book *The Fate of Empires*, Sir John Glubb described six stages in the life of an empire (Figure 13). These stages have analogues in the life cycles of organizations.

■ PIONEER (BIRTH).

Autocratic entrepreneurial leadership characterizes a start-up organization. Many organizations die within the first year due to poor focus, inept management, and weak capitalization. Leadership is more important than management in this stage. When a track record of successes is established, renovation drives the organization toward the stage of Conquest.

■ CONQUEST (ADOLESCENCE).

Leadership continues to be more important than management, but not predominant. This stage is one of physical growth and experimentation, as well as the problems they cause. Employee excitement and morale are high due to innovation, frequent achievement, and being appreciated as team insiders. Sales and market share are emphasized over profits, and the organization becomes an appealing candidate for acquisition. The leaders continually renovate the organization to accommodate its growth.

■ COMMERCE (ADULTHOOD).

Leadership and management alternately share influence in running the organization. Innovation and control are balanced as more interdependent systems and environments affect the character of the whole. Communications are more difficult; key employees have influence, but other employees have little input in decisions or strategies. Quality circles are in place. Strategies for sales, market share, and profit are balanced.

To renew the organization, leaders revitalize with the missionary spirit of the Conquest stage, pulling the organization beyond it to Commercial Conquest. This is not one of Glubb's stages of empire, but mine, to reflect the potential for new growth versus Glubb's deterioration to Affluency and Aristocracy. Without this revitalization, managers begin to have more authority than leaders, and the organization begins to become bigger, rather than better.

- AFFLUENCE (MIDLIFE).
  This is the crisis stage, corresponding to Glubb's Aristocracy, in which profits dominate productivity, managers have more power than leaders, people compete for personal prestige, employment and administrative overhead surge, and bureaucracy expands in size and influence. Equilibrium and status quo are the overriding goals of management, which fails to recognize them as the road to ruin. Because equilibrium stands in the way of productive change, the organization does little more than what is currently acceptable. Hardening of the arteries has begun.

  What is obsolete and aging will soon disappear.
  —HEBREWS 8:13

  Renovation is possible, but an expensive restructuring is more likely to be necessary to rescue the organization. With either strategy, it is the few remaining leaders who must carry it out, while resisting the temptation to get too lean, too fast.

- INTELLECT (OLD AGE).
  "Staff" (the advisors) have significantly more influence than "line" (the doers). Management now dominates, em-

phasizing process over purpose. Those with prestige of position smother the organization with regulations, rules, and manuals. Communication is restricted, innovation and calculated risks are out, decisions are postponed, and remuneration is based solely on position and status. There is an abundance of employees not working at capacity, much less contributing to the organization.

- DECADENCE (DEATH).
  This is the end of the organization—if the process is not halted or reversed at an earlier stage. Leadership is ineffective or nonexistent at maintaining the vision and innovating new strategies; management for the status quo has given the competition a crucial advantage. The organization goes bankrupt and is dissolved, or is taken over by a more powerful organization and sold off in pieces.

ORGANIZATIONAL RESTRUCTURING

Having been witness to, and involved in, organizational renovations and restructuring, I have seen the results of both productive and detrimental leadership decisions. Some of the most important rules for organizational renovation are shown in Table 7.

In 1991, having lost $3.50 per stock share from continuing operations, Tenneco hired Michael Walsh, who had formerly been CEO of the Union Pacific Railroad. Almost immediately, Walsh started a two-year restructuring plan that included a 50-percent cut in the common stock dividend, the sale of $1.1 billion in non-core assets, and a capital expenditure cut of $250 million. In 1992, one year later, Tenneco was reporting a $1.50-per-share gain from continuing operations. Granted, continuing earnings per share are still below the 1990 level, but what a dramatic turnaround!

ORGANIZATIONAL RENOVATION AND RESTRUCTURING

DO	DON'T
1. ENSURE THAT THE ENTIRE ORGANIZATION UNDERSTANDS—AND THE STRATEGY SUPPORTS—THE ORGANIZATION'S VISION, VALUES, AND PRINCIPLES.	1. VIOLATE THE ORGANIZATION'S VALUES OR PRINCIPLES.
2. INVOLVE LINE PEOPLE AND CUSTOMERS IN STRATEGY DEVELOPMENT.	2. CHANGE INFLUENTIAL LEADERSHIP WHILE RESTRUCTURING.
3. PREMEASURE EACH MAJOR STRATEGY PHASE THROUGH THE VALUE EQUATION.	3. ATTACK IN ALL DIRECTIONS AT ONCE OR ENDEAVOR TO GET TOO LEAN TOO FAST.
4. PUT ESSENTIAL AND COMPATIBLE SYSTEMS IN PLACE FIRST, WITH BUILT-IN CAPACITY FOR FLEXIBILITY AND GROWTH.	4. CONVERT NECESSARY VARIABLE COSTS INTO UNNECESSARY FIXED COSTS.
5. DEVELOP EXTERNAL ALLIANCES THAT EXTEND THE ORGANIZATION'S REACH WITHOUT INCREASING ITS SIZE; SHARE USE OF CAPACITIES FOR MUTUAL BENEFIT.	5. RETAIN UNPROFITABLE DEPARTMENTS OR OPERATIONAL CENTERS.
6. PUT THE RIGHT PEOPLE IN THE RIGHT ROLES, WITH CLEARLY DEFINED EXPECTATIONS, AUTHORITY, AND REPORTING LINES.	6. INITIATE EXTERNAL ALLIANCES WITH ORGANIZATIONS THAT ARE NOT COMMITTED TO LONG-TERM MUTUAL BENEFIT.
7. OVERCOMMUNICATE RATHER THAN UNDERCOMMUNICATE.	7. GRANT UNWARRANTED AUTHORITY—AUTHORITY IS BETTER WITHHELD THAN WITHDRAWN.
8. PROVIDE RESOURCES AND TIME FOR TRANSITION TRAINING.	8. CONFUSE ACTIVITIES (MEETINGS, PROCESSES, COMMUNICATIONS) WITH EFFECTIVENESS.
9. CREATE A REWARD SYSTEM THAT RECOGNIZES DESIRED BEHAVIOR AND PERFORMANCE.	9. RETIRE STRONG PERFORMERS OR LEADERS DURING TRANSITION.
10. LAY OFF SURPLUS EMPLOYEES BASED ON PERFORMANCE.	10. UNDERESTIMATE EMPLOYEES' RESISTANCE TO CHANGE.
11. REDUCE EMPLOYEE RESISTANCE TO CHANGE.	

TABLE 7

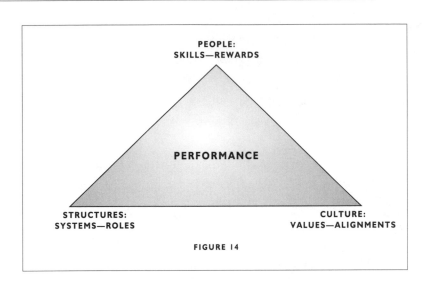

PEOPLE:
SKILLS—REWARDS

PERFORMANCE

STRUCTURES:
SYSTEMS—ROLES

CULTURE:
VALUES—ALIGNMENTS

FIGURE 14

ALIGNING PEOPLE

Organizational renewal is much more than shuffling boxes in the organization's hierarchical chart. After averting capitalization and asset/liability crises as Walsh did, the leader must retrain employees and renew the organization's alliances to improve performance. Performance is the result of the interaction of people, cultures, and structures—a relationship that can be visualized as a triangle (Figure 14).

> *Don't place a Yogi in a Commissar's role.*
> —ANTONY JAY

It is the leader's responsibility to place the right people in the right roles at the right time for exceptional performance, roles that allow them to focus on what they do best. If done for the right reasons and at the right cost, the result can be growth and fulfillment for the individual as well as the organization.

125

HELPING PEOPLE CHANGE

As the environment changes, organizational structures and roles change, and people change; change is the new status quo. But people resist change; it causes discontinuity, disorder, distraction, discomfort, distress; it demands "metanoia" (Greek for "shift of mind and action"). It is better that we choose change than wait until it chooses us—but, regardless, the leader must assess the winds of change and tell the organization what is happening.

> *Change without continuity is chaos. Continuity without change is idleness and deterioration.*
>
> —MAX DE PREE

- RESISTANCE.
  In reducing the organization's inevitable resistance
  to change, the leader—
  - supports and promotes positive change by example and explanation. The leader explains what is causing the change, why it is important, and how it can be made beneficial. The leader channels anxiety into creativity.
  - emphasizes the values providing stability more than the process elements causing instability.
  - tolerates performance short of perfection in higher command decisions, recognizing that a seemingly bad decision could well be the least of evils.
  - communicates what the change will require, and helps the followers develop the skills to meet the new requirements.
  - provides caring during the adjustment period, and discipline if the follower refuses to adjust.
  - demonstrates an appropriate sense of humor.
  - does not let ideals become expectations.

- STRESS.
  Even when the leader does everything right, some followers will internalize, if not externalize, negative stress. This

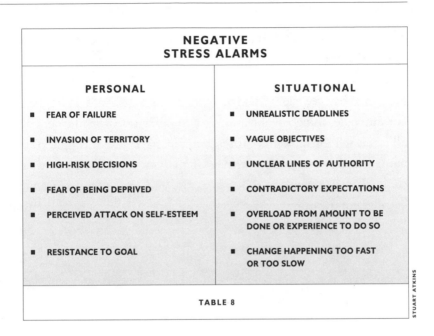

NEGATIVE STRESS ALARMS	
PERSONAL	**SITUATIONAL**
■ FEAR OF FAILURE	■ UNREALISTIC DEADLINES
■ INVASION OF TERRITORY	■ VAGUE OBJECTIVES
■ HIGH-RISK DECISIONS	■ UNCLEAR LINES OF AUTHORITY
■ FEAR OF BEING DEPRIVED	■ CONTRADICTORY EXPECTATIONS
■ PERCEIVED ATTACK ON SELF-ESTEEM	■ OVERLOAD FROM AMOUNT TO BE DONE OR EXPERIENCE TO DO SO
■ RESISTANCE TO GOAL	■ CHANGE HAPPENING TOO FAST OR TOO SLOW

TABLE 8

STUART ATKINS

harmful stress can often be identified through cause-and-effect analysis. Stuart Atkins, author of *Name of Your Game*, provides us with insight into the job-related causes and effects of negative stress (Table 8).

The goal of renovation or restructuring is to revitalize organizational health through—

1. reliable and profitable growth.
2. innovation and creativity for excellence.
3. employee education and contribution.
4. productive internal and external alliances.
5. public acknowledgement of contribution and value.

> *It is one of the most important tasks of command to effect timely and proper change of tactics according to the condition of the terrain and the followers.*
> —SUN TZU

127

Leaders of transformation and renewal, whether through renovation or restructuring, establish purpose, direction, parameters, and an environment for responsible and productive growth. They see the growing organization as a cooperative, collaborative learning organization, an organization with leaders at all levels who inspire and promote applied learning through individuals and teams. Empowerment is the key, through teams that channel interdependent skills, systems, and processes for excellence in contribution.

16

Building and Leading Teams

*Never doubt that a group of thoughtful,
committed citizens can change the world; indeed,
it's the only thing that ever has.* — MARGARET MEAD

TEAM SUCCESS ELEMENTS

Successful teams have four elements in common:

- Purpose, with structures and systems to support that purpose.
- Membership that has the necessary skills and which reflects the diversity of the affected audience.
- Leadership that links and balances the effectiveness of the members with the efficiencies of the system.
- Measures of individual and team performance.

Let's look at each of these more closely.

PURPOSE

The team's purpose is to achieve the goals of short-term projects or to improve ongoing processes. This purpose must always fit the business and mission of the parent organization.

Team structures and systems are evolving and assuming more importance in today's less centralized organizations as they change from vertical hierarchies toward horizontal, process-oriented groups. These new structures require more highly involved and empowered people at all levels. Those who actually do the work have more power to change, create, and contribute to excellence in goods, services, and relationships.

Although Procter and Gamble appears to many to be a strict vertical hierarchical corporation, several of its plants, such as the one in Pineville, Louisiana, have been run by worker teams since the late 1960s. Foresighted leader management in these plants improved profitability and productivity through self-directed worker teams, the implementation of which also addressed the first two of Ken Kovac's important employee needs: employee appreciation, and being considered insiders.

This evolution in team design is described by Wellins, Byham, and Wilson in the book *Empowered Teams*. The effect of this evolution upon team design is shown in two of the authors' charts, from which Table 9 and Figure 15 are derived.

The Team Empowerment Continuum chart is based on a manufacturing team example. It is estimated that fewer than 15 percent of manufacturing teams (even less in other disciplines) of major corporations are self-directed. The change from a vertical, individual-driven structure to a horizontal, group-driven one is not automatic, immediate, or, in many situations, totally desired. Since all organizations are hierarchical to some degree, "self-directed" teams are governed by the level of authority through which the parent organization empowers the team.

KEY DIFFERENCES IN TEAMS OF VERTICAL AND HORIZONTAL ORGANIZATIONS

ELEMENT	VERTICAL	HORIZONTAL
ORGANIZATIONAL STRUCTURE	LAYERED, INDIVIDUAL-DRIVEN	FLAT, TEAM-DRIVEN
JOB DESIGN	NARROW, SINGLE TASK	PROCESS, MULTIPLE TASK
MANAGEMENT ROLE	DIRECT/CONTROL	COACH/FACILITATOR
LEADERSHIP	TOP-DOWN	SHARED WITH TEAM
INFORMATION FLOW	CONTROLLED/LIMITED	OPEN/SHARED
REWARDS	INDIVIDUAL SENIORITY	TEAM-BASED, SKILL-BASED

TABLE 9

EMPOWERED TEAMS, WELLINS, BYHAM AND WILSON

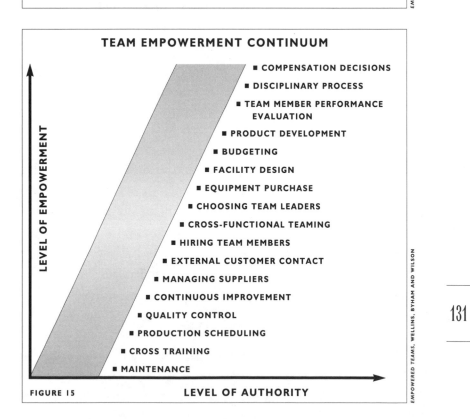

TEAM EMPOWERMENT CONTINUUM

LEVEL OF EMPOWERMENT

- COMPENSATION DECISIONS
- DISCIPLINARY PROCESS
- TEAM MEMBER PERFORMANCE EVALUATION
- PRODUCT DEVELOPMENT
- BUDGETING
- FACILITY DESIGN
- EQUIPMENT PURCHASE
- CHOOSING TEAM LEADERS
- CROSS-FUNCTIONAL TEAMING
- HIRING TEAM MEMBERS
- EXTERNAL CUSTOMER CONTACT
- MANAGING SUPPLIERS
- CONTINUOUS IMPROVEMENT
- QUALITY CONTROL
- PRODUCTION SCHEDULING
- CROSS TRAINING
- MAINTENANCE

FIGURE 15   LEVEL OF AUTHORITY

EMPOWERED TEAMS, WELLINS, BYHAM AND WILSON

131

MEMBERSHIP

Team membership is based upon the compatibility of members' skills with team purpose, and should reflect the diversity of the affected audience.

> *Diversity is the appreciation and development of*
> *individual uniqueness for a common goal.*
> —R. R. THOMAS

Diversity should be a natural variety based on skills and strengths, not a quota system for group entitlement. Successful teams share a common set of principles, values, and purpose in order to channel and capitalize upon individual strengths. Team commonalities are like an adoptive family that understands and embraces the "orphans"—the idiosyncrasies of its members. These teams promote fashion with style: the fashion that states, "Me too," with the style that states, "Only me."

> *Civilization is the recognition and acceptance*
> *of differences.* —Mahatma Gandhi

Team membership comprises primary and secondary members. Primary members (seldom more than 12) are those directly responsible for implementing and fulfilling the purpose of the team. Secondary members (a variable number) are those with expertise in resource areas that are periodically needed. Each member feels valued for his competence, understands the responsibilities of his role, and is committed to excellence.

LEADERSHIP

The initial team leader is assigned by the parent organization; however, as the team evolves along the empowerment continuum, it assumes the authority to elect its own leader. Like all lead-

BOSS TO SUBORDINATE ORIENTATIONS

	STYLES				
AREAS	**IRRATIONAL PRO**	**IRRATIONAL ANTI**	**CONFUSED**	**RATIONAL INSENSITIVE**	**RATIONAL SENSITIVE**
RELATIONSHIP	PATERNALISTIC	ANTAGONISTIC	TENTATIVE	UNCOMFORT-ABLE TO ANTAGONISTIC	MUTUAL TRUST & RESPECT
PERFORMANCE EXPECTA-TIONS	NOT DEMANDING	LOW	UNCLEAR	DEMANDING INSENSITIVE TO DIVERSITY	DEMANDING, YET SENSITIVE TO DIVERSITY
PERFORMANCE FEEDBACK	NEGATIVE FEEDBACK NOT GIVEN	REFLECTS BIAS DEMOTIVATING	INACCURATE	STORES AND DUMPS DATA DEMOTIVATING	ACCURATE ON-GOING GROWTHFUL
DECISION MAKING	UNFAIR	UNFAIR	UNFAIR INCONSISTENT	PROMOTES STATUS QUO	PROMOTES EQUITABLE CHANGE
ADVOCACY	OVER BASED ON GUILT	UNDER BASED ON STEREOTYPES	SPORADIC RESPONSE TO PRESSURE	UNDER FOCUS ON WEAKNESS	MERIT BASED FOCUS ON STRENGTHS

TABLE 10

ers, the team leader coordinates the skills and strengths of team members with the appropriate systems to get the desired results. The leader should not dominate the team; if he does, the team becomes no better than the leader.

Developing cooperative support within the team is among the leader's most challenging assignments. It demands first that the leader be sensitive to members' human needs and behave rationally in order to enroll and align the members with the mission of the team. Then the leader can develop in team members and in himself the skills needed for human effectiveness. This consideration begins with the behavioral appreciation that, before anything else, everyone is a human being. Although the consulting firm Pope and Associates developed the following aid (Table 10) for their diversity seminars, I have found it extremely useful in developing productive team relationships.

The good leader should strive to be a Rational Sensitive with each individual. At times, however, I have exhibited characteristics found in at least two of the other four classifications. For example, as a leader faint in computer literacy, I was a Confused with a team member who was a computer whiz. I seldom gave him adequate lead time, and I was unable to evaluate his performance fairly because I had failed to establish clear performance expectations for him. As a Caucasian male, I have also been an Irrational Pro with both a minority and a female. Without this guidance from Pope and Associates, I might well have continued making these unconscious errors.

TEAM GROWTH STAGES

Productive team building is a transformation process, progressing, regressing, and again progressing through four basic stages (Table 11). The team should understand these stages, and the leader should adopt a style appropriate to the stage. These stages and corresponding leadership styles are similar to the levels of Follower Readiness shown in Table 2.

MEASURES

There are three basic measures of team productivity:

1. EFFECTIVENESS.

   Did the team fulfill its mission or purpose? Did useful innovation occur? Were the members' individual and collective skills enhanced?

2. EFFICIENCY.

   Did the team fulfill its mission on schedule and within budget? Were interdependent systemic costs reduced?

3. RELATIONSHIPS.

   Were internal team relationships improved? Were external alliances developed or improved? Did the team environment improve morale?

LEADERSHIP STYLE FOR FOUR STAGES OF TEAM DEVELOPMENT		
TEAM STAGE	**TEAM**	**LEADER**
1. START UP	HIGH EXPECTATIONS, HIDDEN AGENDAS, ANXIETY, POLITENESS, MINIMUM FEEDBACK AND RISK-TAKING, LITTLE ACCOMPLISHED TOWARD GOALS	AUTOCRATIC (BARBARIAN)— DIAGNOSES, LISTENS, QUESTIONS, DIRECTS, STATES, TELLS
2. NITTY-GRITTY	FORMATION OF CLIQUES, COMPETITION FOR POWER, HIDDEN AGENDAS, CONFLICT, FRUSTRATION	AUTOCRATIC DEMOCRACY (BUILDER)—DEFINES GOALS AND REASONS, IDENTIFIES AND DEALS WITH CONFLICT, COACHES, SELLS
3. COMING TOGETHER	RESOLUTION OF NONPRODUCTIVE STAGE 2 CHARACTERISTICS, OPEN-MINDED PARTICIPATION, HARMONY, CONFIDENCE, USE OF RESOURCES	DEMOCRATIC AUTOCRACY (EXPLORER)—SOLVES PROBLEMS, DELEGATES, DEMONSTRATES, NEGOTIATES, BUILDS CONSENSUS, SUPPORTS
4. THROUGHPUT	UNITY/ESPRIT, PRODUCTIVENESS, POSITIVISM, OWNERSHIP PRIDE, COHESIVENESS, RISK-TAKING	DEMOCRATIC (SYNERGISTIC)— SHARES LEADERSHIP, EMPOWERS, IS INTUITIVE AND INNOVATIVE

TABLE 11

LEADERSHIP DYNAMICS, INC.

The most common mistake leaders make with these measures is evaluating quantity without considering quality.

TEAM MEETINGS

Meetings! Meetings! Meetings! Many are a waste of time—but without them, how can we become a team? The secret lies in the quality of meetings—the productive results, not the quantity. Leaders can enhance the effectiveness of meetings by following the P's, Q, and P checklist:

1. PURPOSE.

   Advise members of the purpose and necessity of the meeting with adequate lead time. Restate them at the start of the meeting. There are three basic types of meetings, each requiring a different leadership role (Table 12). All three

MEETING TYPES			
	INFORMATION	**SITUATIONAL**	**CREATIONAL**
TIME FOCUS	PAST/CURRENT/FUTURE	PAST/CURRENT	FUTURE
PURPOSE	EDUCATION/MOTIVATION	PROBLEM SOLVING	OPPORTUNITY/DISCOVERY
LEADER ROLE	SPEAKER/MODERATOR	PROCESS FACILITATOR	BRAINSTORMING FACILITATOR

TABLE 12

types can be encompassed in a single meeting. The team leader's role must support the purpose of each type.

2. PREPARATION.
   When advising members of the meeting's purpose, give them pertinent information and the agenda topics that will need their contribution or expertise. Request additions to the agenda.

3. PROCEDURE.
   Publish the final agenda, showing time allocated for each topic and the location and length of the meeting. Miscellaneous agenda topics should be last.

4. PROCESSES.
   Use processes such as "flow chart," "fish bone," and "force field" to clearly explain the issues (Figure 16).

5. PARTICIPATION.
   Be patiently attentive to each member's ideas while pushing forward on the issues—"controlled impatience."

6. PROVOKING.
   Use the power of "why," "what if," and "how would you."

7. QUICK.
   Fulfill the meeting's stated purpose and agenda as quickly and constructively as possible without neglecting any topic. Respect each member's time and participation.

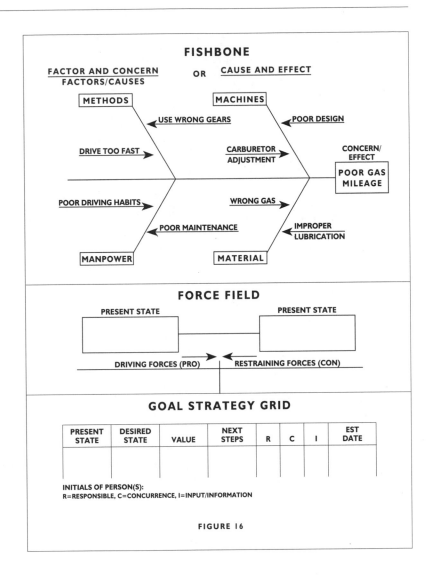

FIGURE 16

8. PROGRESS.

The meeting leader communicates in writing the progress made, the work yet to be done, the person responsible for each piece of work, and the agreed-upon schedule.

"E pluribus unum" ("one out of many") should be the motto of all productive teams!

Growing Leaders
at Work and at Home

I start with the premise that the function of leadership is to produce more leaders, not more followers —RALPH NADER

In *A Force for Change*, author John Kotter illustrates the imbalance in corporate America's leader and manager mix (Table 13):

HOW EXECUTIVES IN A DOZEN SUCCESSFUL U.S. FIRMS RATE THE PEOPLE IN THEIR MANAGERIAL HIERARCHIES		
	WEAK MANAGEMENT	**STRONG MANAGEMENT**
STRONG LEADERSHIP	NEARLY HALF SAY THEY HAVE TOO FEW LIKE THIS	VIRTUALLY ALL REPORT TOO FEW LIKE THIS
WEAK LEADERSHIP	HALF SAY THEY HAVE TOO MANY LIKE THIS	NEARLY TWO-THIRDS REPORT TOO MANY PEOPLE HERE
	TABLE 13	

JOHN KOTTER

DISCOVERY

Leaders grow people! Good leaders nurture growth in all followers, but the nurturing is more challenging, and rewarding, with people who show special leadership potential—people who listen more than they speak, yet to whom others pay attention; people who set examples for others to follow.

As a leader, you will discover these uncommon—and not always obedient—followers by watching their behavior and performance: the quality and quantity of their work, their successes and failures, judgment and learning, creativity and intellect, cooperation and communication. You will see them doing the right things, as well as doing things right, and discover that they have skills and values that are transferable to other endeavors. Perhaps you find that one of your employees, a mother of two, is president of the local PTA. You should consider this person a leadership candidate.

DEVELOPING

Once you have found your potential leader, you should provide greater challenges and risks, classroom and on-the-job learning opportunities, to see if a person has the drive and discipline to become a leader. Cream may rise to the top, but haphazard nurturing slows the process and the payout.

> *No leadership course can affect potential so powerfully as a well-designed sequence of assignments. Not only does it result in new knowledge and skills, it also reduces barriers between divisions and ensures a better flow of information and ideas.*
> —JOHN GARDNER

Few organizations plan well for leadership succession, but those that do, do four things in common:

1. They immediately assign entry-level leadership candidates to established, productive teams and give them responsibility as soon as practical.
2. They place the candidates in predetermined environments with increasing responsibility and risk, and keep them there long enough to enjoy the rewards and learn from their mistakes.
3. They hold formal performance review and goal-setting sessions every six months.
4. They broaden the candidates through horizontal as well as vertical assignments.

Instrumental to this broadening is the candidate's growing understanding of the linkages and balances of the organization's interdependent structures, systems, and processes.

EVALUATION

The performance review and goal-setting sessions are the same as those provided for all followers, but are more frequent for leader candidates. Common elements I have found in successful performance reviews are these:

- An atmosphere that emphasizes the positive.
- Absence of surprises, if the candidate has been given the proper frank and rapid feedback throughout the performance period.
- Specific evaluation of the quality and quantity of performance and behavior in pursuit of mutually agreed-upon objectives, using documented examples and honest, constructive criticism.
- Establishing new objectives and expectations, with scheduling and necessary support specified. Short-term objectives and longer-term expectations for growth and contribution are best limited to two each, so that the focus rises above the clutter of everyday business tasks.

141

Teams now often conduct performance evaluations internally for individual, as well as collective, productivity. This is somewhat more difficult, but the same criteria apply.

Some say performance evaluations should be abolished because they are counterproductive and demeaning. I disagree! When done right, they stimulate the personal and professional growth that can come out of the "carefrontation of compassion." It is not uncommon for anyone, even a leader, to have periods of doubt regarding his performance or his supervisor's assessment. Conversely, evaluations can be counterproductive when they emphasize negatives, avoid specifics, or focus on management by objectives.

MENTORSHIP

The fourth step in leadership development is mentorship, a process conducive to, but not required for, growing leaders. A mentor is a coach who can influence another person's direction of growth. It can be someone outside the organization, or even a peer within; but most often, it is the candidate's immediate supervisor or a leader higher in the organization. Usually it is the mentor who seeks out the candidate to sponsor and support, rather than the other way around.

Strong leaders are mentors and hero builders. They search out potential leaders below them in the hierarchy to coach and support. Without General George C. Marshall, America and its allies might not have fully realized the contributions of Dwight Eisenhower, Omar Bradley, and Mark Clark. General Marshall recognized the potential of and helped these officers long before they achieved the rank of general.

142

> *The final test of a leader is that he leaves behind in*
> *other men the conviction and the will to carry on.*
> —WALTER LIPPMANN

INADEQUATE GROWTH	
CAUSES	**EFFECTS**
■ INADEQUATE SKILL TRAINING ■ UNREALISTIC DEMANDS OR DEADLINES ■ TOO MUCH RESPONSIBILITY, TOO FAST	■ LOW LEVEL OF PERFORMANCE
■ UNCLEAR OR CONTRADICTORY 　EXPECTATIONS ■ NO INPUT INTO EXPECTATIONS ■ LITTLE OR NO CANDID FEEDBACK ■ TOO LITTLE RESPONSIBILITY, TOO SLOW	■ LOW LEVEL OF DESIRE 　OR INTEREST
■ MANAGER CONFLICT ■ EMPHASIS ON NEGATIVE RECOGNITION ■ EXTENDED PERIODS OF OVERLY 　LONG HOURS ■ LOCATION OR ROLE CONFLICT	■ PERCEPTION OF BEING HELD 　IN LOW LEVEL OF ESTEEM

LEADERSHIP DYNAMICS, INC.

TABLE 14

To varying degrees, each of these four leadership development steps is as applicable in the family as in other environments. Why do some with potential not develop as expected? The causes and effects are similar in all environments (Table 14).

LEADERSHIP DEVELOPMENT AT HOME

Leadership development and training begin in the family. It is the parents' example that establishes the first standards for the child's behavior.

> *Train a child in the way he should go; and when he is older, he will not turn from it.*
> —PROVERBS 22:6

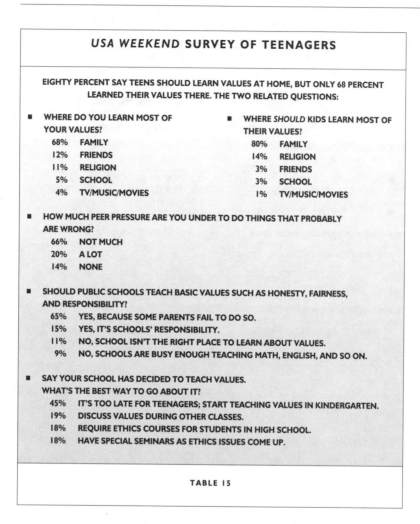

USA WEEKEND SURVEY OF TEENAGERS

EIGHTY PERCENT SAY TEENS SHOULD LEARN VALUES AT HOME, BUT ONLY 68 PERCENT
LEARNED THEIR VALUES THERE. THE TWO RELATED QUESTIONS:

- WHERE DO YOU LEARN MOST OF YOUR VALUES?
  - 68% FAMILY
  - 12% FRIENDS
  - 11% RELIGION
  - 5% SCHOOL
  - 4% TV/MUSIC/MOVIES

- WHERE *SHOULD* KIDS LEARN MOST OF THEIR VALUES?
  - 80% FAMILY
  - 14% RELIGION
  - 3% FRIENDS
  - 3% SCHOOL
  - 1% TV/MUSIC/MOVIES

- HOW MUCH PEER PRESSURE ARE YOU UNDER TO DO THINGS THAT PROBABLY ARE WRONG?
  - 66% NOT MUCH
  - 20% A LOT
  - 14% NONE

- SHOULD PUBLIC SCHOOLS TEACH BASIC VALUES SUCH AS HONESTY, FAIRNESS, AND RESPONSIBILITY?
  - 65% YES, BECAUSE SOME PARENTS FAIL TO DO SO.
  - 15% YES, IT'S SCHOOLS' RESPONSIBILITY.
  - 11% NO, SCHOOL ISN'T THE RIGHT PLACE TO LEARN ABOUT VALUES.
  - 9% NO, SCHOOLS ARE BUSY ENOUGH TEACHING MATH, ENGLISH, AND SO ON.

- SAY YOUR SCHOOL HAS DECIDED TO TEACH VALUES. WHAT'S THE BEST WAY TO GO ABOUT IT?
  - 45% IT'S TOO LATE FOR TEENAGERS; START TEACHING VALUES IN KINDERGARTEN.
  - 19% DISCUSS VALUES DURING OTHER CLASSES.
  - 18% REQUIRE ETHICS COURSES FOR STUDENTS IN HIGH SCHOOL.
  - 18% HAVE SPECIAL SEMINARS AS ETHICS ISSUES COME UP.

TABLE 15

Reports to the contrary notwithstanding, most teenagers know the importance of values. The preceding data are from a 1992 *USA Weekend* survey of 126,000 teenagers (Table 15).

PARENTAL RESPONSIBILITY

These survey results support my stance that the greatest single leadership responsibility lies in being a parent, and that positive values taught in the home should be reinforced by teachers in schools and churches. They also support my faith in, and optimism for, the future. For the most part, we adults are performing more than adequately, but we need to pull and push more aggressively toward excellence.

Parental leadership is mentorship at its finest. Although my family will quickly attest to my shortcomings as a parental expert, I do know that parents and teachers need to exercise loving discipline, set good examples, and enthusiastically share values, principles, expectations, and hope, qualities that are infinitely more important than quantitative materialism, and which can shape the character of a child long before the child completely understands them.

True sharing is difficult, because it reveals the vulnerability of the sharer. At the risk of displaying my own vulnerability to you, as I have to my children, I share two of the major roadblocks in my leadership development within my family. These weaknesses were (and to a lesser extent, are) impatience and overprotectionism. Fortunately, I recognized them early and began trying to explain them to my children well before they could fully understand.

My impatience was directed more at our son, Rip. I wrote the following poem for and to Rip; it reflects a scenario that never happened, but for which I certainly provided opportunities.

JUST A VERY FEW MOMENTS—PLEASE

Don't bother me!
I can't spare the time right now!
I'm busy—why don't you see?
Go away, do something else somehow!
    But Dad, an answer to a question I need
    For there is something I want to do.
    Oh well, your command I will heed,
    I'm sorry, I didn't mean to bother you.
Why won't he give me time for my thoughts?

I'm so busy—doesn't he understand?
A thousand questions he has brought.
Why is it my time he should so inconsiderately demand?
    I guess Dad doesn't really care.
    I'll just go on and do it anyway.
    Since he doesn't have the time to spare.
    If I am wrong, what can he say?
Why did my boy do that thing?
He is old enough—he should know
The trouble that something like that would bring!
Someday—maybe someday—
out of this foolishness he will grow.
    I don't know why I did it.
    At the time I thought it would be fun;
    I didn't think anyone could be hit,
    When I aimed that empty gun.

How often have we, as leaders, failed to be sensitive to and patient with our followers' needs? In our minds these needs may seem unimportant, but our followers may need an attentive audience. They will get that audience with us, or with others. When they feel they must go to someone else, we have lost some degree of leadership effectiveness.

It took me longer to recognize my overprotectionism; but when I did, I shared the following with Jaynanne:

WOMAN/CHILD

When it is in my power to nurture your
    moments of happiness—
I will do so
Were it in my power to shelter you from all pain—
    I would not do so

For how then would you appreciate and enjoy
    your happiness?
When it is in my power to help bring simplicity
    to your world of complexity—
      I will do so
Were it in my power to provide you total stability
    or security—
      I would not do so
For then how would you continue to grow
    and become the complete person you can,
    and ought to be?
When it is in my power to be there for you—
      I will be
But if I refuse to be there, it is not because
    I want to
For you, too, must have your space to test yourself,
    to succeed, and yet—
      sometimes to fall short
To face yourself and proudly acclaim how good
    and beautiful you are—
      as well as how much more you can be
You, my woman child of the universe, have
    given much to me—
      helping me understand what I also can be
We have the mutual treasure of love and
    understanding—
      what more could I ask?

    Risks and mistakes are valuable lessons in the joy and pain of growth. Without them, there would be little learning or innovation, and even less contribution. Leaders encourage calculated risks and well-intentioned mistakes, for they know that without them there is little constructive action and no growth.

147

> *We must not only build the future for our youth,*
> *but, more importantly, we must build our youth*
> *for the future.* —FRANKLIN D. ROOSEVELT

There is nothing magical about leadership. It is contributing to today and building for a brighter tomorrow cooperatively through others who are responsibly and productively doing what they want to do while becoming who they want to be.

A LEADER'S PRAYER

Your seas are great, my ship is small;
Give me the strength to fight our betrayer's call
You are God, I am but man;
Guide me through troubled waters, when You can.
Allow Your love to become my main mast so that
    upon the waves
Justness and kindness I shall cast.
Through my voyage, allow me to share
With those less fortunate in their fare.
Sound the fathom before I erringly yaw,
So that I won't crash upon the reef of Your Law.
Fill my sails when the wind is light;
Give me courage and faith, when I feel fright.
Your stars, not passing ships, for direction I need
When through unchartered waters I choose to lead.
Thank You for showing me the uncommon way;
Through Your help, I will be stronger this day!
Behold this day, for it is ours to make!

Bibliography

Adizes, Ichak. *Corporate Life Cycles*. Englewood Cliffs,
New Jersey: Prentice-Hall, 1989.

Althaus, Paul. *Ethics of Martin Luther*. Philadelphia: Fortress
Press, 1972.

Atkins, Stuart. *The Name of Your Game*. Beverly Hills: Ellis
& Stewart, 1981.

Bach, Richard. *Jonathan Livingston Seagull*. New York:
Avon, 1973.

Barker, Joel Arthur. *Future Edge*. New York: William Morrow
and Company, 1992.

Bass, Bernard M. *Leadership and Performance Beyond
Expectations*. New York: Macmillan, 1985.

Becker, Ernest. *The Denial of Death*. New York:
Free Press, 1973.

Belasco, James A., and Ralph C. Stayer. *Flight of the Buffalo*.
New York: Warner Books, 1993.

Bellman, Geoffrey M. *Getting Things Done When You're Not
in Charge*. San Francisco: Berrett-Koehler Publishers, 1992.

Bennis, Warren. *On Becoming a Leader*. New York:
Addison-Wesley, 1989.

Bennis, Warren. *Why Leaders Can't Lead*. San Francisco:
Jossey-Bass, 1990.

Bennis, Warren, & Bert Nanus. *Leaders*. New York: Harper
& Row, 1985.

Blanchard, Kenneth. *Leadership and the One-Minute Manager*.
New York: William Morrow and Company, 1985.

Boesch, Paul. *Much of Me in Each of These*. Houston:
Premier, 1966.

Bothwell, Lin. *The Art of Leadership*. Englewood Cliffs, New Jersey: Prentice-Hall, 1988.

Branch, Harlee. "The Crowd and the Common Place." Speech in Atlanta, 1971.

Cantor, Dorothy, and Toni Bernay. *Women in Power*. Boston: Houghton Mifflin, 1992.

Caroselli, Marlene. *The Language of Leadership*. Amherst, Mass.: Human Resource Development Press, 1990.

Cohen, William A. *The Art of the Leader*. Englewood Cliffs, New Jersey: Prentice-Hall, 1990.

Covey, Stephen R. *The Seven Habits of Highly Effective People*. New York: Simon and Schuster, 1989.

Davis, Burke. *Marine*. Canada: Little & Brown, 1962.

DePree, Max. *Leadership Is an Art*. New York: Dell, 1989.

DePree, Max. *Leadership Jazz*. New York: Doubleday & Co., 1992.

Dilenschneider, Robert L. *A Briefing for Leaders*. New York: Harper Collins, 1992.

Drucker, Peter. *The Practice of Management*. New York: Harper, 1954.

Frankl, Viktor E. *Man's Search for Meaning*. New York: Simon and Schuster, 1984.

Frankl, Viktor E. *The Will To Meaning*. Meridian, 1988.

Franklin, Benjamin. *Franklin: The Autobiography and Other Writings*. New York: Viking, 1986.

Gardner, John. *On Leadership*. New York: Macmillan, 1990.

Glubb, John. *The Fate of Empires*. London: Blackwood, 1981.

Griffith, Samuel B. *Sun Tzu, The Art of War*. New York: Clarendon, 1963.

Haas, Howard G. *The Leader Within*. New York: Harper Collins, 1992.

Hackworth, David. *About Face: The Odyssey of an American Warrior*. New York: Simon and Schuster, 1989.

Helgesen, Sally. *The Female Advantage*. New York:
    Doubleday & Co., 1990.

Holmes, Paul. "Surviving Crisis." *Marketing Week*,
    March 27, 1989.

Hough, Richard. *Winston and Clementine*. New York:
    Bantam, 1990.

Howard, Jane. *Margaret Mead: A Life*. New York:
    Ballantine, 1985.

Iacocca, Lee. *Iacocca: An Autobiography*. New York:
    Bantam, 1984.

Jay, Antony. *Management and Machiavelli*. New York:
    Holt, Rinehart, and Winston, 1968.

Kanter, Rosabeth Moss. *The Challenge of Organizational
    Change*. New York: Macmillan, 1992.

Kotter, John P. *A Force for Change*. New York: Macmillan, 1990.

Kotter, John P. *The Leadership Factor*. New York:
    Macmillan, 1988.

Kouzes, James M., and Barry Z. Posner. *The Leadership
    Challenge*. San Francisco: Jossey-Bass, 1987.

Macay, Harvey. *Swim with the Sharks*. New York:
    William Morrow and Company, 1988.

Manz, Charles C., and Henry P. Sims. *Super-Leadership*.
    New York: Prentice-Hall, 1990.

McCullough, David. *Truman*. New York: Simon
    and Schuster, 1992.

McLean, J. W., and William Weitzel. *Leadership: Magic,
    Myth, or Method*. New York: AMACOM, 1991.

Miller, Lawrence M. *Barbarians to Bureaucrats*. New York:
    Random House, 1990.

Murphy, Emmet C. *The Genius of Sitting Bull*. Englewood
    Cliffs, New Jersey: Prentice-Hall, 1993.

Musashi, Miyamato. *A Book of Five Rings*. New York: Over-
    look Press, 1974.

Naisbitt, John, and Patricia Aburdene. *Megatrends 2000: Ten New Directions for the 1990's*. New York: William Morrow and Company, 1990.

Peters, Tom. *Thriving on Chaos*. New York: Alfred A. Knopf, 1987.

Phillips, Donald T. *Lincoln on Leadership*. New York: Warner Books, 1992.

Roberts, Wess. *Leadership Secrets of Attila the Hun*. New York: Warner Books, 1989.

Roosevelt, Theodore. "The Man in the Arena." Speech in Paris, 1910.

Rowan, Roy. *The Intuitive Manager*. Boston: Little, Brown & Company, 1986.

Sayles, Leonard P. *The Working Leader*. New York: Macmillan, 1993.

Schutz, Will. *The Truth Option*. New York: Ten Speed Press, 1984.

Senge, Peter M. *The Fifth Discipline*. New York: Doubleday & Co., 1990.

Siegel, Irving. *Parental Belief Systems*. Hillsdale, N.J.: Erlbaum, 1985.

Thomas, Roosevelt R. *Beyond Race and Gender*. New York: AMACOM, 1991.

Toffler, Alvin. *Future Shock*. New York: Random House, 1970.

Untemeyer, Louis. *The Road Not Taken*. New York: Simon and Schuster, 1970.

Von Clausewitz, Carl. *On War*. London: Penguin, 1968.

Walsh, Michael. "Finding New Heroes for a New Era." *Fortune Magazine*, January 25, 1993.

Washington, Booker. *Up from Slavery*. Williamstown, Mass.: Corner House, 1971.

Wellins, Richard S., W. C. Byham, and J. M. Wilson. *Empowered Teams*. San Francisco: Jossey-Bass, 1991.

Wilson, Larry. *Changing the Game*. New York: Simon and Schuster, 1988.

Zaleznik, Abraham. *The Managerial Mystique*. New York: Harper & Row, 1989.

Index

Leadership Dynamics, Inc.

Leadership Dynamics, Inc. is a consulting firm
with one core mission:

To assist and mentor others in discovering, developing, and delivering upon their unique leadership potential.

Joe Reynolds, the principal of the firm, earned his degree in industrial management from Samford University. He learned and honed his leadership skills in large organizations such as the U.S. Marine Corps and Procter & Gamble. Joe had 30 years' experience in sales management with Procter & Gamble before founding Leadership Dynamics. He is a member of the National Speaker Association.

To inquire about speeches, seminars,
and consulting provided by Leadership Dynamics, contact:

Mr. Joe Reynolds, President
Leadership Dynamics, Inc.
4314 Cypresswood Drive, Spring, Texas 77388

713-353-3155

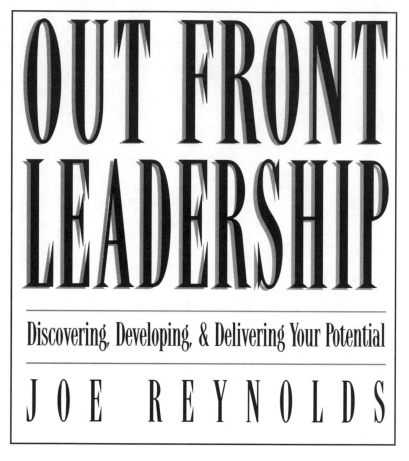

OUT FRONT LEADERSHIP

Discovering, Developing, & Delivering Your Potential

JOE REYNOLDS